The Vatican
and Eastern Europe

The Vatican and Eastern Europe

WILFRIED DAIM

Translated by Alexander Gode

Frederick Ungar Publishing Co.
New York

Translated from the original German,
Der Vatikan und der Osten,
by arrangement with Europa-Verlag, Vienna

Preface

The Catholic Church finds itself at a juncture requiring ruthless honesty. Nothing less assures it credibility in the "world."

The Church is about to carry out fundamental changes. Many of its dignitaries refuse to see this. They promote an image of the Church with room for continuities but not for leaps and shocking shifts, for flowing transitions but not for cataracts. In this sense it was claimed that John XXIII merely continued the work of Pius XII or, in fact, "completed" it.

Changes of basic significance are doubtless underway in the realm of Church-political realities, too, and this entails contradictions which confuse the faithful in the absence of reliable and frank information. Those outside the Church do not see clearly either. Enlightenment is needed, honest enlightenment. We cannot afford to gloss over better insights because standing up to them entails the admission that things we thought or believed in the past were wrong.

The refusal to admit past errors is a type of dishonesty which derives from an expanded claim to infallibility. This must be revised in favor of a more modest and simultaneously more realistic attitude.

It is the objective of this book to help Catholics and non-Catholics to recover their sense of direction as they strive to understand the happenings and crises within the Church.

Wilfried Daim

Contents

The Vatican
and Eastern Europe

Introduction

The phrase "politics of the Vatican" has uneasy overtones. Many Catholics deny outright that such a thing exists. This hails from unrealistic concepts. Politics of the Church has been around since the time of Constantine.

The politics* of the Vatican thus has its tradition. To be sure, in the course of the centuries not only the methods and techniques underwent changes but also a considerable portion of the objectives. Since the days of Pius XI, for instance, the restitution of the Pontifical State has been given up. Other objectives have remained, and new ones have emerged. It is quite difficult to understand the workings of the politics of the Vatican, and in fact no attempt has ever been made to explain it in its totality.

Then, too, there is no moral theology to support the politics of the Vatican or, more precisely, the politics of the Church. Is it right, for instance, would it be right, in view of the re-introduction of religious instruction in the schools of Poland, to recognize the Oder-Neisse line as the permanent Polish-German frontier? Was it right for Leo XIII to forbid the Poles in an encyclical of his to rebel against Russian rule with the explanation that the czar in St. Petersburg was the "legitimate authority" to whom obedience was due, just because he, Leo XIII, was hoping he might

---

* Translator's note: It will be noted in the following pages that repeatedly the term "politics" appears where a more elegant construction would have been possible through the use of the term "policies." This calls for the following explanation: The western European languages—with the exception of English—think of a policy as a singular unit of politics and of politics as a plurality of policies, and use the same term for both concepts. Much that Wilfried Daim says cogently about politics would have become diffuse, had he had to say it in a language discriminating between policies and politics. The translator chose to preserve Daim's cogency by attempting to operate without the term "policies."

1

thus win over the czar to the cause of the pontifical state? Was
it right for German bishops to support Hitler's war in the east,
just because those in power there were atheists? Was it right to
disregard the Polish concordat in the matter of establishing the
jurisdiction of German bishops in the Warta basin because there
seemed reason to hope that Hitler would allow Catholic missionary work in the east? Is it right for Vatican diplomacy to utilize
the devices—conscious lies, for instance—that are unfortunately
favored by secular diplomacy for reasons of prestige and the like?

All these are moral questions which the official moral theology
of the Church has never raised and certainly not answered. If
we consult in this matter the chapter "Church and State, Church
and Politics" in the relevant standard work by Bernhard Häring,[1] we come away with extremely vague impressions, although
there are some passages there which seem to criticize, at least by
implication, positions that were at one time held by the Pope.
For instance:

> This indicates that anyone violates the true essential mission of the
> Church when he strives to obtain for it positions of secular power or
> attempts to draw it into the secular affairs of politics as such.
>
> Nothing, however, is thus said against the Pontifical State in its
> present form, for that state surely represents no position of power but
> rather the protection of the independence of the Pope from all
> possible encroachments of a political power. Similarly, the totally
> nonpartisan attempts at mediation of the Apostolic See and its endeav-
> ors to restore peace do not in any way conflict with the mission and
> the spiritual character of the Church.[2]

In this passage Häring suggests indirectly that the principles
formulated in the first paragraph do support the argument
against the pontifical state as it once was but not against it in its
present form. But he does so with all the delicacy known to be
useful to a man inside the apparatus of the Church.

Yet even when the politics of the Church is backed neither by
fear nor an expansive power drive, it is admittedly extremely
difficult to see in the individual concrete case where the limits lie.
That is the reason they have been drawn so very differently.

Since 1917 the Church has been confronted with a new phenomenon. First there was one state and today there are several states in which atheism is a kind of state religion and in which religious denominations are at best accorded a greater or lesser degree of tolerance. Looked at from a vantage point in Italy and hence from that of the Vatican, all these states are in the "east."

There is between atheism and the doctrine of the Catholic Church a greater theoretical difference than between Catholicism and any previous anti-Catholic regime, be it Christian-heretical, Mohammedan, or pagan. The one regime most nearly comparable to communism in its antiecclesiastic attitudes is possibly that of the French Revolution. Consciously atheistic regimes are to Christian consciousness an extreme and largely novel phenomenon. This is the reason Vatican politics cannot follow in this matter a schematic routine. Still, there are various analogous experiences in the past of the Church, and the present confrontation is by no means as unique as one may be inclined to assume.

There is also the fact that communism did not find or create a clean slate in any of the countries in which it came to power. Many of the aspects of Soviet communism belong in the historical continuity of the czarist empire. Particularly the geographic and ethnic traditions have undergone but little change. It would therefore be quite wrong to minimize components of long-standing continuity because of the new element of atheism.

The view sometimes held in the Federal German Republic that the establishment of a pro-Soviet regime in the former Soviet zone of occupation was an act of specifically communist inspiration can be taken seriously only by those who believe that if Germany had attacked a liberal or feudal Russia, such a Russia, being ultimately victorious, would simply have withdrawn its troops. On the basis of historical analyses one would rightly expect that a liberal or feudal Russian regime would have acted essentially as the Soviets did.

Again, it would be totally wrong to regard the differences between the Polish communist government and Cardinal Wyszynski as representing a specifically Catholic-communist conflict, for there are concepts of Polish politics that are older than communism. Every attempt to bring about an understanding between

Pope and czar—regardless of whether the initiative came from the Vatican or from St. Petersburg—was looked at askance by the Polish conservatives. Should this no longer be so today?

Politics, it appears, must be broken down into its various component determinants. This applies obviously to the politics of the Vatican, too. Like every other type of activity, politics is determined by multifactorial causes. Indeed, any type of activity that is political in a special sense requires a highly differentiated evaluation of the total field, with due consideration of the most varied contributing causes.

The complexity of the subject is such that the most detailed analysis cannot hope to do justice to all its facets. Simplification was not just desirable but inescapable. Furthermore, the necessary information was not always available. At times, lacking documents had to be replaced by a logical processing of indirect evidence. The author will consider his self-assigned mission accomplished if he has succeeded in showing at least some of the most essential determinants and in thus contributing to a better understanding of the highly complex events and constellations of facts.

Politics

The concept of politics can be taken in a broader and in a narrower sense. In the scientific delineation of concepts everyday usage should not be dealt with in so arbitrary a fashion that nothing or little remains of its acceptations. It is surprising how rarely works of political science define the word "politics" and, when they do, how little the definition coincides with the meaning of the word in common usage. Scientific concepts should be sharper, more precisely delineated, and narrower than those of prescientific parlance but not completely different.

Political behavior has a number of distinctive characteristics. These include a certain sophistication of anticipation and the ability to embrace the most diverse factors in the overall calculation. But a mode of action that is well thought through does not always and of necessity deserve to be called political. It is only an action within the framework of a human society that can assume political significance. And the components which need to be paid heed to are primarily human components: human conditions, human institutions. In this sense there is cultural politics, there is politics of economics, there is politics of the Church. When objectives within society are being aimed at, the implication is always that favorable forces must be mobilized while forces of interference must be inhibited.

There can be no doubt but that this entails in all cases an element of power. However, we should refrain from mystifying this term, for it is rare that power turns into an end in itself, although among men this case can occur, too, for with men a great many things can turn into ends in themselves. As a rule, however, the possibility of arranging and of deciding is being aimed at because those involved are inspired by the desire to achieve specific objectives which they expect to be benefited by

5

the process. A man can want to make money in order to achieve influence, and he can want to achieve influence in order to make money. A man inspired by the idea that he wants abstract art to be predominant, that is, "ruling," in a given country can strive to achieve this objective by endeavoring to become his country's minister of education.

In a qualitative sense the term "political" implies special skill in the endeavor to achieve certain objectives within society. Yet, in the widest sense every mode of action is to be regarded as political if it aims at attaining goals within society. This, then, calls for the supplementary characterization of politics by various possible attributes: politics can be skillful, clumsy, astute, dumb, naive, narrow-minded, and so on.

In the analysis of the politics (or policies) pursued by an individual or an establishment it is hence necessary to distinguish a series of factors, including the actors (the individuals pursuing the politics), the objectives, and the methods (or perhaps better the techniques). The term "method" implies here rather the theoretical procedures concerned with the achievement of understanding while the concept "technique" comprises the practical procedures of implementation. Both terms share an element of systematic planning, most frequently in marked subordination to a rational approach.

As one looks at a given form of politics from these points of view—not neglecting the fact that the objective may very well be the defense of the status quo—one cannot but increase one's understanding of it. And that is our primary goal. As we proceed in our study, we will find that the situation is in reality much more complicated than has here been postulated. Yet, the factors mentioned so far—actors, objectives, and methods (or techniques)—do suffice to provide the broad frame of reference called for at this time.

Politics
of the Vatican

Catholic and non-Catholic puritans often maintain that there should be no such thing as "politics of the Church" or "politics of the Vatican," for Christ said that his kingdom was "not of this world." If, however, we use the terms "politics" and "political" in the inclusive sense of common parlance as expounded in the preceding chapter, we cannot but conclude that Jesus of Nazareth did indeed engage in politics. His way of dealing with Caiphas was clearly political, that is to say, methodically planned, including his own death which he no doubt expected.

Of course, we may think of "politics"—in keeping with a variant in usage—as covering activities concerned with structural aspects of society and societies in the "secular," as contrasted with the "spiritual," realm. In this sense, the term "political" could not be applied for instance to the activities of a group of bishops striving systematically to undermine the power of a cardinal of the Roman Curia. But even if we reserve the use of the word "politics" to activities in the "secular" realm, we will run into serious difficulties as we strive to differentiate between the realms of the "secular" and the "spiritual." Of course, the existence of such difficulties is no argument one way or the other.

The struggle between politicans and priests can be amply documented throughout history, making quite clear that this is not specifically a problem of modern times. There were conflicts between "the two kingdoms" in ancient Egypt, in the empire of Genghis Khan, in the Middle Ages of the Western world, and they reappear in the differences between state and party in the Soviet Union. If it were possible to devise a precise differentiation of what is "secular" from what is "spiritual," it would—by implication—be clear when and under what conditions the

Church may "engage in politics." Unfortunately, the differentiation is no simple matter at all.

Surely, the "purpose in being" (the *raison d'être*) of all ecclesiastic groups—at least according to the traditional Christian doctrine—is ultimately the eternal salvation of the individual and possibly of groups of individuals. But the decision regarding such salvation is reached here on earth, in this world. Hence, the behavior of the individual toward his neighbor, that is to say, his social behavior, has a bearing on eternity, on his salvation. Problems of society, the "decent" Christian demeanor of the individual within the framework of society, thus come to assume great "spiritual" significance.

In a—relatively speaking—static society, it is easier—compared to a dynamic society undergoing rapid changes—to derive seemingly dependable norms from Jesus' central commandment: "Love thy neighbor as thyself." In the days before the French and the American revolutions, the guiding principles of the then prevailing "Christian doctrine of society" were perhaps not fully convincing, but they could be repeated often enough: "Masters, be good masters. Slaves, be good slaves." This meant: Masters, keep busy giving alms . . . Serfs, don't begrudge your masters' wealth, behave yourselves nicely, for all authority comes from God . . . And that sort of thing. However, when at the time of the Second Vatican Council several German bishops tried to present Erhard's "social market economy" as a timely implementation of the principle "Love thy neighbor as thyself," their arguments did not sound particularly convincing, and they met with embarrassing skepticism.

That one should be as "good" as possible within the limits of one's possibilities, is no doubt a Christian precept. But whether the prevailing social system must simply be accepted as "God-given," is another question. There can be differences of opinion as to what constitutes the maximally possible implementation of principles willed by God. Christianity does establish primary principles of ethics and morals, but their application in the realm of practical realities is subject to far-reaching differences of interpretation even among experts. Here begins an area where the clergy must defer to laity.

The situation is further complicated by the fact that in any given society only a segment of those belonging to it professes to be Christian, acknowledging the validity of the Christian code of morals and accepting the authority of the Church. Can one, for instance, if one happens to be in the majority, demand of Mohammedans, Jews, and atheists that they must abide by the Catholic regulations regarding the day of the Lord, marital morality, and the like?

Here the problem becomes weighty. The question of the freedom of conscience begins to loom over the horizon. If a given society includes groups governed by diverse sets of absolute values, an order must be created that allows them the possibility of a free development and entails no coercion in any sense. This implies that a common base must be looked for which will enable each of the groups to observe its own distinct moral precepts. We have entered an area of secular, communal, and—ultimately—political features in which conditions must be such that it will be possible to live under them as a non-Christian no less than as a Christian.

Protestants in Italy at present must observe the Catholic marriage laws although Protestant teachings would permit them for instance to obtain a divorce. If there were state laws on divorce, they could not, of course, prevent the Catholic from *not* obtaining a divorce. (An exception might be state-imposed divorce proceedings, such as might obtain in the case of racially mixed marriages in a country under a racist regime.) But it is no doubt easier for many Catholics to live up to the principles of their own Church in a society in which divorce is forbidden than in one which permits it. But is this enough to justify one group imposing its will on others?

To escape this dilemma, the totalitarian wing within the Church argues as follows. It demands that state law be organized in accordance with "natural law" based in turn on "natural reason." It then invariably comes about that the analysis guided by what is called "natural reason" leads to formulations in keeping with the truths of Christian revelations (which in fact represent distinctively Christian values), with the result that in the end non-Christians are after all made to submit to Catholic norms. In Italy the Catholic Church continues to demand marital laws based on Catholic principles of marital morality, and this in spite of the fact that the axiom of religious freedom is officially recognized.

But how far can one go in recognizing freedom of conscience? To take an example, a portion of a given society may well hold that the interruption of pregnancy is not to be equated with murder. Even extremely liberal Catholics, who—while they feel personally bound by the principles of the sanctity of the sabbath, the indissolubility of marriage, and the like—do not wish to impose their tenets in such matters on others, will have grave qualms in regard to the sanction of artificial interruptions of pregnancy. With a modicum of good will, solutions can be found in extreme cases. It is quite imaginable, for instance, that non-Catholics, out of deference to their Catholic fellows, would make the interruption of pregnancy a punishable act (except in cases in which the continuation of pregnancy would threaten the life of the mother), while simultaneously institutions would be established for the care of unwanted children and while the sale of contraceptives would be legalized. The fact that a given denomination opposes the use of such devices as far as its own members are concerned does not imply that those who do use them are guilty of murder. Such practices are not to the same extent an insult to the individual's conscience. On the other hand, if we assume that one group regards the killing of a minority as justified, all the others would have to prevent it from implementing that conception, for killing *is* murder and does constitute an extreme insult to the individual's conscience.

If there is to be freedom in the individual's adherence to a religious group, then that group must not raise its own laws to the level of state law even if it includes the great majority or even if all the members of the state belong to it, for the individual must retain the free possibility of severing his relationship with the religious group. A Christian who respects his non-Christian fellows will hence be satisfied with a state that permits him to live in accordance with Christian principles. He will not, on the other hand, demand that Christian principles be imposed on non-Christians. In keeping with this, he will in the face of new and unexpected developments refrain from insisting that only a very specialized manner of responding to those developments can be regarded as Christian. Even the most honest endeavor to be fair to others cannot remove the problem. The thought that it is possible in each and every case to draw a precise line between politics and religion is fallacious.

The politics of the Vatican is politics on a world scale (except possibly where the attitude of the Vatican in matters of Italian domestic politics is concerned, this being an area of special interest to the Vatican). On a world scale Catholicism of course cannot lay claim to a position of predominance. Seen internationally, the Catholics are a minority. Then, too, the Catholic hierarchy has no armed forces, and the sovereign state of Vatican City is fortunately not more than a midget. Yet in the international constellation prevailing at present, military power is to a large extent only a potentially significant factor of world politics. In a labile situation, a minority can assume a world role of great significance. For these and many other reasons, the politics of the Vatican has come to be a matter of great importance. Simultaneously, to be sure, it is undergoing changes that can only be termed revolutionary. Although—as mentioned—there are many Church functionaries who keep clinging to the pretense of a continuity which does not exist, even the most conservative and reactionary writers begin to wake up to the fact that Vatican politics is no longer based on the concepts of the age of Pius XII.

Objectives

As one considers the question of the objectives of the politics of the Vatican, it might seem that there can be no doubts and no uncertainties in this matter. After all, how could there be an objective of the politics of the Vatican other than the spread of Christianity? This implies that the Vatican must favor a political situation which promotes such a spread.

In fact the primary interest of Vatican politics is characterized in this way. There are, of course, secondary interests, which are to serve the primary interest by indirection, such as for instance the endeavor to provide the Church with a favorable economic basis.

Ultimately the primary interest of the Church is the maintenance of a base of operations that is maximally advantageous to its expansion, and this is the point to which it comes back time and again. In this way the Oder-Neisse line and its recognition are of concern to the Church above all as objects of its primary interest. To the Church it is a secondary question whether Germans or Poles live in the territory east of the Oder-Neisse line. The only important point is whether Catholics live there. The politics of the Church is hence conditioned by the question as to whether and how far the recognition of the Oder-Neisse line meets its primary interest. If it seems possible that negotiations with political agencies in Poland will yield results profitable in terms of the primary interest of the Church, the recognition of the line will be favored. There is, naturally, the further delicate point that in the process the German Catholics must neither be lost nor unduly antagonized.

The primary interest of the Church raises a number of problems. There is no clear single answer to the question what the situation in a given state should be to provide maximally favorable conditions for the expansion of Catholicism. It is possible to set up a "scale of attitudes toward the Church" which individual states may assume. Let us construct such a scale beginning with the extremely negative and winding up with the maximally positive attitude:

1. The Church is the object of an active and radical persecution by the state (in ancient Rome during the era of the Emperors or—at times—in communist states).
2. The Church is rejected by the state and treated with extreme reserve (in certain communist states).
3. The Church is being treated neutrally by the state (in certain Western democracies).
4. The Church is being treated benevolently by the state (in the Federal Republic of Germany and in Austria).
5. The Church is recognized by the state as the prevailing ideological power, while non-Catholic denominations are being treated with marked reserve (in Spain and in Austria during the Dollfuss-Schuschnigg era).

6. The Church is recognized by the state as the dominant ideological power, while all other creeds are being persecuted (in various states during the Middle Ages).

A great many Catholics will refuse to consider the situation of the last two levels as "especially or maximally favorable" to the Church. From the point of view of these Catholics it hence cannot be a primary interest of the Church to strive to bring about such a situation.

In fact the ideas of the Vatican in this respect have undergone a change. As recently as in the thirties and during the era of Pius XII the notion prevailed that a negative attitude of the state toward other creeds and atheism had to be striven for as being advantageous in terms of the primary interest of the Church. During the Second Vatican Council lively discussions were concerned with the problem of the freedom of faith and of conscience. Spokesmen of reaction and conservativism, especially from Spain and Italy (Ruffini, Ottaviani, and others), were of the opinion that the true religion could not possibly be treated on a par with false religions.[3] In this the fact is overlooked that the situation imposes a choice between a community of convinced Christians and one of individuals whose creed is imposed by coercion. It goes without saying that precisely the same people who have no objection to Christianity by coercion demand tolerance for the Church.

There are numerous non-Catholics who fear that the Church would not be able to resist the temptation of curtailing the freedom of others if it were given such a possibility by being conceded the corresponding position within a state. The truly progressive wing of Catholics—among them no doubt John XXIII (and possibly Paul VI as well)—will feel that a neutral or benevolent attitude of the state toward the Church is most advantageous to the latter's primary interest. After all, it is only when the Church is freely allowed to proclaim the Gospel, while simultaneously no one is coerced or forced to join the Church that the possibility prevails of winning over the largest possible number of human individuals as convinced followers. This disposes of the fear still prevalent in lay circles lest the Church might find its way back to terror, implying the imposition of its principles on others by means of the help of the state.

Paul VI has repeatedly declared that the Church is intent on "serving the world," implying that it does not strive to rule. When we consider the historical past of the Church, we do not find it difficult to understand the concern of the laity. Pope John XXIII was so convincingly "non-pro-terror" that he won cordial sympathies outside the domain of the Church as well, and as a result a great many members of the clergy, though—to be sure—not the dyed-in-the-wool reactionaries in the hierarchy, became convinced of the need for genuine tolerance. Paul VI, by contrast, gives the impression that he wishes to return to a more autocratic attitude, as witness in particular his encyclical *Humanae vitae*. This was apparent already during the Vatican Council when he repeatedly imposed his will on the "episcopal brethren." However, this attitude—at least so far—has remained restricted on the whole to internal matters of the Church.

The Church does have the possibility of demonstrating beyond the shadow of a doubt that it is exclusively interested in a neutral or benevolent attitude on the part of the state by renouncing of its own free will its position of dominance in countries—such as Spain, for instance—where it does occupy such a position. During the Second Vatican Council there was in fact evidence that the understanding was gaining ground that such a development would promote the primary interest of the Church. There are, indeed, not a few Spaniards who see this point. On the other hand, members of the Spanish hierarchy appear to fear that there will be mass defection once the Church is no longer backed by state pressure. This risk is of course quite real, for under changed premises numerous opportunists would cease to be Catholics. On the other hand, it is a question whether this would really be so very harmful, for it would merely make manifest the latently existing defection from Catholicism. Illusions would be lost but no genuine values.

In truth, numerous Catholics have begun to wonder how it was at all possible that in a church whose core commandment is the love of neighbor such intolerance should have come to gain a foothold. Why was it that the Church strove in the first place to assure itself the massive support of the state?

At this point a few basically significant observations on the Vatican seem called for. In one of the loggias of the offices of the Cardinal Secretary of State there is a large fresco representing the map of the world going back to the sixteenth century. Many of its details are no doubt incorrect, but it does show that global and indeed universal thinking prevailed at the Vatican at a very early time. National particularisms—with the possible exception of Italian nationalism—are beneath the level of the Vatican.

However, this global thinking has a double motivation. One root of it is the Christian universality deriving from Jesus' precept, "Go yet therefore and make disciples of all the nations." It is a message of brotherliness, implying an ultimate equality of all, but was not propagated in this spirit. Rome did become the center of Christianity, but this did not signify that the Christian principle of brotherliness had conquered Rome. It merely meant that the old pagan clans had accepted baptism and had managed in exchange to take over the Papacy within a very short space of time. This is how Roman imperialism gained a foothold in the innermost interior of the Church. It is extremely difficult to expel it again. A serious attempt in this sense was not undertaken before John XXIII.[4]

This Roman imperialism is likewise universal in its thinking, but in the sense of rule and hegemony. Vatican diplomacy is thus a combination of Christian universality and Roman imperialism. The latter—seen functionally—has numerous advantages, if we disregard the dignity of men as "God's children," who —from the point of view of the papal imperator—must be "subjected." The Romans did regard most other peoples as barbarians and themselves as the "master race" (although theirs was never as primitive a racism as that of let us say the National Socialists). They knew full well that not only the Romans could fight but also the Parthians, Nubians, Slavs, Teutons, and Mongols. But they also understood that it was possible for Rome to use the barbarians as pawns in a game played for high stakes of power. There is a trace of this feeling of superiority in the attitude of an Italian monsignore toward the bishops in the "misty north" [5] and the countries beyond the great water, and he prides himself with being able to "deal with them."

From Roman imperialism the Vatican inherited political "wisdom," sophistication, foresight and circumspection, the ability to wait, but also a condescending sense of superiority and a pronounced lack of understanding for democratic and socio-communal endeavors and for everything egalitarian and ultimately fraternalistic. Basically the clergy, imbued with Roman imperialism, is convinced that social problems can be resolved only in terms of rule and subjection. If the reproach is made that this conflicts with Christian love, the reply will come that it is precisely through ruling that the priest serves his flock, for his "service" consists in ruling. An analogous phenomenon is the symbiosis into which Great-Russian czarist imperialism has entered with Marxism, making it ultimately possible for the Kremlin to argue that the occupation of the Czechoslovak people's democracy by Soviet troops represented a "service" to the people of Czechoslovakia.

This ideology of rulership has the effect that an ecclesiastic hierarchy imbued with it prefers forms of political organization to which it can issue directives but which are ready to take on by themselves the dirty business of devising appropriate administrative measures to lead dissenters, heretics, and atheists back into the embrace of Holy Mother Church. In this manner those wretched creatures are "served" best, although of course they are unable to really sense this.

It would be utterly wrong to believe that Vatican politics is today determined in all its facets by Roman imperialism. But it would be equally wrong to believe that this frame of mind is now truly and completely a matter of the past. It simply isn't. In particular, it isn't within the Holy Office, as witness for instance the affair of the book, *The Human Mystery of Sexuality* ["Le mystère humain de la sexualité"] by Marc Oraison. The Holy Office—whose changed name emphasizes most innocently its competence in "questions of faith and morals" (in which connection it is difficult not to think of the name changes from

Cheka to Ogpu to NKVD to MVD)—did not place the book on the Index but forbade instead all future publications by the author.

If the "Congregation for Questions of Faith and Morals" pursues such a course in interior politics it may be assumed that it will respond in a similar way in matters involving international relations, though its procedures would doubtless be more carefully camouflaged. Indeed, it is not difficult to understand the fear prevailing outside the Church with respect to its further expansion. After all, by turning toward Catholicism a man runs the risk of being treated as Marc Oraison was treated. The suspicion is not far-fetched that the Church will undertake the attempt to increase its powers when the state assumes toward it an attitude of neutrality or even benevolence. When in the Federal Republic of Germany Hochhuth's play *Der Stellvertreter* [The Deputy] was put on the stage, there was indeed a trend favoring the use of the powers of the state to suppress this statement of opinion of a Protestant Christian.

Still, it would be far off the mark to assume that the Vatican is indeed striving to arrogate to itself a world rulership over man in his entirety and is but waiting, in ambush as it were, for an opportunity to establish its rule of tyranny. It would be equally naive to postulate that the Kremlin or the White House is harboring such intentions. In both these institutions there are imperialists, but in both there are also individuals of a different turn of mind.

The Second Vatican Council has opened the doors to liberalism. It is not liberalism as a formally declared principle of policy but it has provided some elbow room for those to whom respect for the freedom of man implies that—as a matter of principle—they cannot want more than an ideologically neutral state. Such a state can lend support to the Church but must simultaneously be ready to lend support to other denominations and to atheists as well. When the Church has the freedom to proselytize yet does not attempt to achieve conversions by coercion with the help of the state, it will win over to its side individuals inspired by genuine conviction. It is possible that the final outcome will be a smaller number of Catholics, but these will be better Catholics, and instead of Catholics by coercion there will be non-Catholics who have not been deprived of their human dignity.

However unfair it may be when Christians violate the spiritual freedom of others, it is also unfair and likewise an insult to man's sense of humanity—albeit perhaps to a lesser degree—when atheists and non-Christians declare the Church to be an institution of non-freedom. However, suppression by atheists cannot be judged by the standards which apply to suppression by Christians, for atheists do not operate under the commandment of brotherly love.

If in the Soviet Union the Church is granted by the constitution "freedom of worship" and the atheists "freedom of antireligious propaganda," this cannot be called "freedom of conscience," unless one is ready to share the (unhumane) posture of the old "Congregation of the Holy Office." For the faithful are allowed to speak within the Church and the atheists outside of it. This may sound formally equivalent, but there is in fact so great a difference that quantity—as Marxian dialectics has it —does become quality.

In sum, then, the objective of the politics of the Vatican to see states established which assume toward the Church an attitude of neutrality or benevolence must be regarded as totally justified. Recalling the experience of various states in their dealings with the Church, it is simultaneously impossible not to sympathize with the desire of such states to prevent the Church from promoting political conditions that can be exploited to the disadvantage of non-Catholics. The Church must be prepared in this respect to accept criticism and frank accountings.

As an argument against the still widespread distrust of the Vatican there is the cogent point that it is outside the realm of factual possibilities that there should ever be a Catholic-authoritarian regime on an international scale.

While the Vatican may strive for the establishment of political conditions under which the states assume toward the Church an attitude of neutrality as a minimum requirement or at best are ready to recognize it as the predominant ideological power, the most likely development is one involving an attitude of neutrality or benevolence toward the Church.

This much about the primary interest of the Church. What, now, about its secondary interests?

Marxists can hardly be expected to see that in the last analysis the Church is not conditioned by economic factors. To be sure, economics plays a more or less important role in the life of any man. Some human individuals reduce that role to a minimum. The best example is that of the prophet John the Baptist who went into the wilderness where his raiment was of camel's hair and his food locusts and wild honey. Men who ostentatiously establish their independence of the economy frequently come in contact with others to whom "giving is joy." As a result they can afford economically to stand up against kings.

Jesus sent his disciples (as apostles and bishops) among men and sent them without the burden of earthly possessions, for those hearing them would care for them out of a sense of moral responsibility. And the disciples did not have to go hungry. Jesus had been quite right in expecting that their economic independence would strengthen the power of conviction of their words. The "superstructure" is the more autonomous, the narrower its economic base.

Constantine imposed upon the Church fetters of gold. Feudalism and the penetration of Roman imperialism added their bits to make within the Church the bondage of material property a factor of extraordinary strength. Yet, the spirit of poverty lived on in the Church, and reformers "from within," such as St. Francis of Assisi, embodied in this sense the inner conscience of the Church.

But it was a characteristic of the feudal system that the styles of life of masters and subjects be separated by a gulf, and so also the styles of life of the bishops and their flocks. The bishops needed palaces, and the display of wealth in which the Churches became involved "to the greater glory of God" was often unheard of.

The feudal attitudes of the princes of the Church resulted in their feeling it to be "beneath their dignity" to be supported by the people, for that implied a dependence which injured the sensitivities of high lords and masters. How could one be expected to depend on the "free will" of those whom one felt called upon to rule? Should, for instance, a primate of Hungary "go begging" among the faithful or is it not "worthier" of him when he lives on the revenue from Church properties?

Today the Church drags along a heavy burden of feudal belongings the preservation of which requires enormous sums. In many instances there is no way of utilizing such possessions in an economically meaningful fashion. Even if the Vatican were willing, it could not, for instance, sell a Michelangelo statue to buyers abroad without arousing in the Italian people high waves of understandable excitement. Here lies the reason the Church has had to turn over to the state old monasteries and houses of worship both in Italy and in France in order to assure the preservation of significant works of art. Then, too, the Church owns extensive real estate: vineyards originally built up for the sake of the celebration of the Mass and forests and fields. Many monastic establishments have enough land to support from its revenue twenty times the number of monks affiliated with them.

The chains of gold of the Church are indeed heavy and burdensome. On the other hand, the Vatican needs a great deal of money for its missionary activities. And finally, it must take care of the economic security of the Church in future times. Hence its holdings in bonds and other negotiable instruments.

But it is possible to find solutions that would be economically satisfactory without impairing the political freedom of movement of the Church. It is imaginable that the state would take care of genuine cultural monuments, while the Church would decide to live on the liberal gifts of the faithful. The transition would be difficult, but such a solution would doubtless be the best. After all, as things are today forty per cent of the needs of the Vatican are covered by voluntary gifts of the Catholics of the United States, although in that country the Catholics do not represent the wealthiest strata of society. There can be no doubt but that political decisions of the Vatican are at times partly or even decisively determined by economic considerations, though only in the rarest cases exclusively so. States which are hostile to the Church now have the possibility of using economic sanctions to bring the Church to heel. But precisely when that happens, it becomes apparent how much genuine religious substance there really is of a kind not subject to damage by economic collapse and disaster. This is a fact of convincing portent. Furthermore, a reduction in the Church budget of nonessentials implies an increase in essentials, particularly in freedom.

When state and Church and, similarly, hierarchy and flock are interlinked by a relationship of trust, many prollems can be solved. For instance: the Austrian state and the city of Vienna derive considerable revenue from tourists who come to see the Cathedral of St. Stephen. This makes it reasonable that the state and city should contribute to the extremely costly maintenance of that structure. But such a contribution by secular agencies would not justify the transformation of churches into museums.

From all this it is apparent that economics is important to the Vatican and that it opens the doors to all sorts of influences which one would prefer to see kept out. But despite these facts, economics should not be assigned an absolute role. Economic motives are ends in themselves only in extreme cases, though they do virtually always enter into the picture as more or less important contributory factors. If now the attempt has to be made to cut loose from one social system and establish connections with another, it follows that new economic bases must be looked for, although it will always be a difficult problem to cast off the economic fetters of the old system. It will be difficult but certainly not impossible.

Methods

Vatican politics has today no military backing that could in any sense be taken seriously. In fact, the papal army never represented a convincing power. The knights of the Teutonic Order in the north did constitute an impressive fighting force, but to regard them as a papal army in a strict sense seems hardly possible, for the Order pursued to a large extent its own politics. The popes had to use for their purposes the armies of other Christian states. This means that they could act militarily only by indirection. In any event, the Vatican could call for crusades and put Christian princes under moral pressure.

As recently as 1938, at the Eucharistic Congress in Budapest, the later Pope Pius XII—then Nuncio and Papal Legate Pacelli —could propose in well-turned allusions a crusade against bolshevism. While this proves that the most recent instance in which the idea of a crusade came to the fore is by no means a matter of the distant past, it is also to be noted that the idea had sufficiently fallen into disrepute for Nuncio Pacelli to feel obliged to limit himself to recommending it by circuitous suggestions. To be sure, there have always been politicians who could not be impressed by anything less than the sword. The last important representative of this frame of mind was Stalin. His ironical question, "How many divisions does the Pope have?" does not precisely testify to a deep understanding of the power of peaceful means. On the other hand, I remember a Soviet journalist who said to me in Moscow: "We do have divisions, and so do the Americans. But these divisions are not used, with the result that someone who has none or only a very few—Nehru for instance—can play a major part. The Pope, perhaps, too." [6]

When we think of attempts to turn the wheel of history back and to restore Roman imperialism to its old position of power within the Church, we cannot but consider it a great advantage of Catholicism over communism that the Pope has no tanks, at least none that are made of steel. The tanks he does have are sublimated. This, if it does nothing else, makes it impossible for him to try to stop the developments within the Church in as infantile and primitive a fashion as the Kremlin tries to arrest the development of communism: witness its occupation of Czechoslovakia. A papal occupation of the Netherlands—the Czechoslovakia of Catholicism—is impossible because there are no tanks of steel. The result is that seen as a rival of communism, Catholicism has the better chances of evolution. In both situations, however, the principle remains valid: No counterrevolution restores the *status quo ante rebellionem*.

There can be no doubt but that few or none of those with influence inside the Vatican still harbor ideas of crusading. A modern crusade against communism would of necessity turn into an atomic war. On the one hand, the inhumanity and, in the last analysis, un-Christianity of war has penetrated the conscience of those responsible to a much larger extent than held true in ages past, and, on the other hand, a war—particularly an atomic war— would result in the survival of so small a minority of men that missionary work among them would not really be profitable in terms of the "economy" of the care of souls.

What is left, then, is the attempt to exert an influence on the governments and the peoples in the various countries of the world. The possibilities of exerting such an influence must not be underrated. To be sure, there are marked differences from case to case, both with respect to the possible objectives and with respect to the type of person that can be approached. On an international scale, the influence the Vatican can exert is certainly significant. Yet, a total, that is, a determining influence (in a specific question) can never involve more than a restricted circle of individuals. When the Vatican wants to address an appeal to the Catholic laity or to the bishops of the Church, the subject must be of a kind which by general consensus falls within the range of its competency. On the other hand, when the bishops can invoke their moral authority, their influence reaches not only the Catholic laity but a great many non-Catholics as well. John XXIII, whose love of man was said to be genuine far beyond the range of Catholicism, is an example of the international influence which the Vatican can exert.

Hitler recognized the importance of Vatican decisions and concluded for that reason a concordat with the Vatican shortly after his seizure of power. He could do so light-heartedly, for he never intended to live up to the agreement. All those who tend to equate National Socialism and communism should recall the lengthy negotiations between Yugoslavia and the Vatican in matters of the "concordat-like treaty" which was finally signed in Belgrade in 1966. Tito would never have gotten himself involved in such protracted discussions if—like Adolf Hitler—he had regarded the outcome as no more than a "shred of paper."

Hitler's concordat was advantageous to the Third Reich both domestically and in the field of international politics. To be sure, Germany's Catholics were not revolutionary, but an organized minority need not be revolutionary in the full sense of the term to represent a major risk for an authoritarian regime. A stand explicitly condemning the murder of Jews and other "racially inferior individuals" and the declaration that the soldier's oath on Hitler was sheer blasphemy would have had repercussions far beyond the immediate sphere of influence of the Church. In particular, the true believers among the Protestants would have regarded such a papal pronouncement, though addressed specifically to the Catholics, as a serious appeal to their consciences, too. In fact, it is likely that even the "indifferent"— those abiding by no religious rules—would have rejected the killing of Jews if it had been called "brute murder" with no mitigating mincing of words and would have sabotaged the system. Hitler's concordat with the Vatican paralyzed not only Catholic resistance but beyond that the resistance of Protestants, liberals, and others. In addition, it made Hitler "socially acceptable" in the halls of international politics.

This makes clear what great importance must be ascribed to the Vatican's seal of approval and moral endorsement and explains why this importance is by no means restricted to the core of truly committed Catholics. In a constellation of labile balance in particular, the influence the Vatican can exert may prove extraordinarily significant. Relative to communism, the Vatican has the possibility of opening and closing at will the ideological "police line." We are probably not far off the mark when we suggest that the Vatican's decision to take the Soviet profession of peaceful intentions seriously obliged even Konrad Adenauer to recognize that the Russians were "no longer" in a mood for war.

In terms of international politics we must finally mention how the Vatican has repeatedly made use of the possibility of "dropping" political affiliates and of shifting its own position. In 1933, for instance, the Vatican "dropped" the German Center Party in favor of Hitler. In 1938 it "dropped" the Austrian *Quadragesimo Anno* state of Schuschnigg (letting it be engulfed in the *Anschluss*). It "dropped" monarchies, too. It "dropped" Franco, and in 1966 it "dropped" the Christian Democratic Union in the Federal Republic of Germany.

In order to veil its shifts in position, the Vatican generally tries to give the impression that it never acted in any other way. It also strives, whenever possible, to cushion the blow for whoever gets dropped. In 1938, in the case of Austria, nothing of the sort could be done, but after 1945 Kurt Schuschnigg could be paid the smart money of being invited to lecture during the Catholic University Weeks. Konrad Adenauer was given as a salve the Order of Christ. A particularly impressive illustration of the point here under discussion is the treatment that was meted out to Portugal. The country has a century-old history of unrelenting support of Catholic missionary work, such as for instance in India. The enclave of Goa remained for a while, after the establishment of an independent India, a colony under Portuguese rule—until Nehru had it occupied. Since the Second World War the Vatican has come to understand that the times of the supremacy of the white race and of colonialism are definitely passed. The rigid attitude of Portugal in the colonial question is as hopeless in the long run as the racism of the South Africans. Beyond that, the primary interest of the Vatican requires that the new states, the young peoples of the "third world," be given support. Although Spain and Portugal did a great deal for the Church during the centuries of their colonial expansion, the Vatican today sees no reasons why they should not be "dropped," for they have become weak.

Paul VI went to Bombay, signifying indirectly that the Vatican recognizes the new state of affairs. The conservative Portuguese and Salazar in particular made no bones about their feelings in this matter. Was this not "treason" on the part of the Vatican toward its allies? It isn't enough to be conservative, one must be naive to expect the Vatican to be true to its friends "till death does them part." The Vatican shift was not meant to alienate the Portuguese; it was meant to win over the Indians. What then could be done to assure the Portuguese of the Pope's good will? A way out was found. Paul VI sent a golden rose to Fátima, officially honoring the national shrine of Our Lady of the Rosary. To be sure, this was not much of a trade-in allowance on Goa, but it was at least an expression of condolence. Such little tokens of social amenity are skillfully managed at the Vatican. It would be a challenging assignment for courageous moral theologians to study the question how such an attitude of "diplomacy" is compatible with the eighth commandment or Jesus' words: "But let your speech be, Yea, yea; Nay, nay: and whatsoever is more than these is of the evil one." In any event, the bestowal of such honors can cushion the fall of those whom the Vatican "drops."

The bascule technique is a revealing feature of Vatican diplomacy and deserves to be studied with great care. Examples of it are found time and again, particularly in the area of Church politics relative to the East. At times, to be sure, the Vatican overrates its influence on the Catholics and even the lower clergy. This was apparent when Leo XIII wished to win over the czar to a pro-Vatican political course and sought for this purpose to induce the Poles to submit to the "legitimate" czarist rule. This was something the Poles were not ready to buy, and they decided instead to rebel. This reaction had not been taken into consideration in the Vatican's calculations. A moral authority can exert a certain degree of moral influence, but there is no guarantee that this influence will become factually manifest. There have been numerous instances in which the moral influence of the Vatican was indeed a political reality. The most militant anticommunists in the Federal Republic of Germany—the right-wing factions in the Christian Democratic Union—faced considerable difficulties as a result of the politics of the Vatican toward the eastern states, for it seemed somehow absurd that in their condemnation of the atheists they should outdo the Pope, trying as it were to gild the gold refined at Rome.

All in all, then, the point here to be made is that the influence of the Vatican is doubtless a reality but that in the individual case it is difficult to appraise it in quantitative terms. Furthermore, the range of variability of this influence depends more on subjective determinants than on objective facts. In any event, it is wise not to underrate the importance of acts and actions of the Vatican, particularly when one has the impression that their motivation is Christian in a deeper sense of the term.

"Eastern" Politics
of the Vatican

The reason the word "eastern" appears here in quotes is that it will be used and is to be understood in the following pages in its colloquial and unscientifically imprecise sense. As a rule, when we speak of an East-West conflict, we mean the conflict of communism and capitalism or that of the "un-free" and "free" worlds. To be sure, when Radhakrishnan explained at Oxford that communism was after all no "eastern" product but one of the "West," he was reasonably correct, if one looks at things in historical terms. Then, too, there are many eastern states which are by no means communist, such as, for instance, certain Arab countries, India, and others. Yet in common journalistic parlance, the term "East" refers to those countries in which communism is in power. In this sense Cuba belongs to the East. Of course, such an interpretation is somewhat primitive, for the political coherence of this "East" is rather dubious. What is there today, we may well ask, that unites China and Soviet Russia? Even if the two powers continue to share certain features, it certainly is not possible to use the same political approach to China as to Soviet Russia.

The present discussion will not be concerned with the politics of the Vatican with respect to China and Albania. This restriction seems justified in the light of the foregoing and also because there is as yet little to be said on this score. Pope Paul VI's statement for the United Nations that those countries not yet belonging to that organization should join it was obviously meant to be an allusion to China. In back of this there is a neutralist concept in the sense of the third world, but this concept is far from clear at the present time. Indeed, it could hardly be expected to be clear in view of the impenetrable events in present-day China. Our theme, then, is the politics of the Vatican relative to the

European communist countries (with the exception of Albania).

Two aspects of the theme deserve to be studied separately: The ideological aspect, that is to say, the coming to grips of the Vatican with communism as an ideology, and the historical aspect, which closely depends on the historical conditions prevailing in the various countries. After all, the Vatican had a political attitude toward Russia long before communist atheism came into being. And the "eastern" politics of the Vatican entails components which have nothing to do with communism and whose effects and implications are today more or less what they were in the past. To be sure, these historical aspects differ from one country to the other, while communism is—relatively speaking—a constant entity, although its manifestations likewise differ with the historical backgrounds of the individual nations.

The Problem of Communism

Communism confronts the politics of the Vatican with a difficult problem. Yet, it would be erroneous to claim that there are no historical analogies to this undoubtedly extraordinary challenge. Such an analogy may be seen in Mohammedanism which for a long time seemed to represent a mortal threat to Christianity, while Protestantism, too, represented a similar threat to the Catholic Church. It is possible to object that these historical analogies cannot be considered as such because their ideological content had nothing to do with atheism. But there was also a French Revolution which led to a republican system of statehood based to a large extent on an atheistic ideology. This point will have to be discussed in greater detail in a later context.

For the present a few brief remarks are called for concerning the relationship of Christianity and the Christian Church to the various social classes.[7] Nietzsche maintained that the Jews had more categorically than anyone else declared war on masters, men of eminence, and men in power, with the implied stipulation that the lower and lowly are the truly good, pious, and blessed in God. Moses called himself a descendant of slaves. The prophets and ultimately Jesus of Nazareth, too, represented the lower strata of society.[8] This argument seems cogent, and so does Nietzsche's thesis of Christianity as "a religion of untouch-ables." The nobility of Rome regarded Christianity as somehow plebian and as hence constituting a threat to Roman imperial-ism.

There were other religions in imperial Rome that bestowed their friendship on the slaves, but among these Christianity was doubtless the most important. It responded to the suppression it experienced by establishing still stronger ties with the lowly, the "underdogs." This does not imply that it was the objective of Christianity to destroy the prevailing upper classes. It rather strove to establish a universal brotherhood and thus to abolish the differences between the high and the low. However, the Con-stantinian turn maneuvered the Church into a position of con-servatism,[9] with the result that the forces of social reform and social revolution left the Church or took refuge along the cir-cumference of the domain of the Church where it was possible to tolerate them—and to ignore them.

When the bourgeoisie won out against feudalism it did so, on the one hand, on the basis of Christian-heretical ideologies and, on the other hand, with the help of anti-Christian systems of thought. The first breakthrough against British feudalism oc-curred in the United States of America on a Christian-heretical basis, while the feudalism in France was undermined by an anti-Christian or rather anticlerical ideology. This latter point is readily understood, for the high clergy was through and through feudalistic. It identified itself with the monarchic system and sought to justify this identification on the basis of Christian prin-ciples.[10] From the point of view of conservative Catholicism, the association of feudal monarchy and Church seemed so close and so necessary that the alliance of "throne and altar" was regarded as insoluble. The hierarchy of the Church and the nobility of the state seemed as though created for the purpose of a joint rule "by the grace of God." In terms of fact all this is utter non-sense, for basically Christianity and feudalism are ideologically incompatible and could be interlinked only by the distortion of basic Christian truths. On the other hand, particularly in Europe, the affiliation of anti-Christian atheism with republican democratism likewise came to be regarded as natural and necessary. To find the association historically understandable is one thing, but to regard the argument as cogent is another. A monarchist can very well be an atheist, and a republican can be a Christian.

Despite the victory of reaction throughout Europe, people with a flair for realities recognized long before the end of the nineteenth century that the idea of the republican democracy would ultimately prevail over that of the monarchy. The Vatican understood the implications of the situation and acted accordingly. Leo XIII "dropped" the royalists in France and accepted the theses of the much-maligned Catholic republicans. This means that he bestowed his favors on the bourgeoisie. The nobility still occupied important positions of power which induced the Pope to veil the shift in his position by the bestowal of orders and other amenities involving neither commitment nor obligation.

The neutral attitude of the Vatican toward feudalism and the republic of the bourgeoisie was in the last analysis a desertion to the opposition. The position of the Vatican in this transitional situation was that of a broad-minded father who through his liberal understanding finds a place in his heart both for the progressive reformer (whose victory is thereby promoted) and for the old-line conservative. The firm foundation on which the monarchic system was built up was not, after all, represented by the handful of noblemen but rather by the masses of Catholics who—contrary to their class interests—felt in their consciences bound and obligated to their princely rulers. The relaxation of the ideological tension between Church and republic resulted in a breaking of the dam which had kept the Catholic masses from acting in accordance with their class interests. What all this really meant was that the Vatican had "dropped" the monarchy. For a while the Catholic population in its greater part kept faith with its traditional obligations. Only a small minority promptly left the old camp, but precisely this small minority could tip the scales in a labile situation.

In the Federal Republic of Germany, for instance, the Catholic bishops had been supporting the Christian Democratic Union directly and massively in its stand against socialism up to the time of the elections to the regional diets in 1966. However, in its declaration relative to the elections in the Land of North Rhine-Westphalia, the episcopate maintained a strict neutrality, which did not mean too much to the great majority of the Catholics who well remembered the earlier declarations in favor of the Christian Democratic Union, but it did weaken their conviction that nothing other than the Christian Democratic Union could possibly be accepted. Indeed, a small marginal segment deserted to the Socialist Party, which was enough to give it a majority in the popular vote. There obviously were other reasons to account for this election upset, but there can be no doubt but that many Catholics had lost their inhibitions about casting their votes for the Socialists.

This situation opens up a grand opportunity for socialism, provided the socialists understand the situation. A politics of good will toward the Church can strengthen the power of the socialists and increase their majority by a considerable margin. To be sure, one must not expect as yet an explicit endorsement of socialism by the Church. Such a development will take time. For the present the Church will continue to pretend that nothing has changed. When the Church changes its mind, it does so slowly and gradually and almost imperceptibly.

In speaking of the identification of the Church with a particular class we must make a distinction between the ideology of that class (which may be more or less anti-Christian) and its social system. Through its scholastic training the Church is a past master in such distinctions insofar as its direct interests are involved. In the present instance the distinction to be made is that between liberalism as a bourgeois ideology and the democratic-republican form of social organization. One may predict that the response of the social group with which the Church is about to come to terms will be a positive response. This may not be immediately apparent but will be so in the long run. The group involved needs time, too, to overcome its distrust, but it is bound to recognize that it is about to lose an adversary and to win new support, this latter specifically in its pursuit of its most important political objective, which is—in one sense or another—the rebuilding of the prevailing social system.

It stands to reason that the Vatican in its dealings with communism must utilize—in ideological contact with the Catholic left—the same methods which it once used in dealing with liberalism. The militant hostility to religion which characterizes communism does represent an extremely serious problem for the Church. Yet, the ultimate objective must be to change communism from an antireligious into a proreligious movement. To be sure, this can only be a long-term objective. It can only be reached through a protracted process involving various phases and stages. The militant aggressive hostility may first lose its active component and become an attitude of cool detachment. This may then evolve into tolerance to the point of neutrality, the latter of a kind no longer incompatible with good will.

To be sure, the complexity of such a development involves the fact that an institution like the Roman Curia is a complex bureaucracy which must not be thought of as monolithic in any sense. There may be total agreement among its factions as to the ultimate primary interests of the Church but not with respect to the evaluation of the prevailing situation and its inherent possibilities.

For instance, when Leo XIII effected the shift from the Church's profeudalism to its endorsement of middle-class democracy, the protagonists of feudalism inside the Vatican did not suddenly disappear. There can be no doubt but that in Leo's times there were groups in the Vatican that worked and spoke against any kind of arrangement with the French republic because they regarded a democracy as the work of the devil and hence condemned it.

But what was the solution of the republican-democratic problem as seen by such conservatives? There was no real chance of restoring the Bourbons to power. There was nothing left but the hope for a miracle, and the only instrumentalities for its implementation were crusades of prayer.

At the other extreme there were liberal French Catholics with a leftist program. Their aim was a reconciliation with the democratic republic on the basis of an identification of the Church with the republic against the monarchy. However, even if Leo XIII had favored such a course, he would have had to proceed via a neutral intermediate phase during which a Christian could be a republican as well as (or at least almost as well as) a monarchist.

Today the pendulum has gone the other way. It is still possible —for there is no law that forbids us to be fools—to be a Catholic and a monarchist, but this can be done only at the price of living behind the times. As for France, the leftist concept of reconciliation opened up new long-term prospects for an expansion of the Church. Since he understood the concrete reality of this chance, Leo veered toward the left, and—as witness the subsequent historical developments—in doing so he did the right thing. Today liberalism has largely abandoned its former hostility to religion. The parties of the bourgeoisie, now called conservative, consist primarily of Christians. This applies, for instance, to the Christian Democratic Union and also to the Austrian People's Party. What is important in all this is the fact that the Vatican opted in its strategy not for an irrational-conservative group but for a group of rational progressivism, for the simple reason that the latter had a rational concept and did not base itself on irrational mysticism.

Similar groupings exist naturally inside the Vatican relative to the politics of the Vatican toward communism. Here again the conservatives have a conceptually clear program, and that means that they can be factored out of the calculations. What, then, are the concrete possibilities? One can want to destroy communism, modify it, or allow it to evolve. Its destruction as a power system could be achieved only at the cost of an atomic war. Its modification implies the need for a revolution. Both these possibilities are rejected by the Vatican. There remains, then, the possibility to hope for an evolution in the course of which the communist system will become liberalized and humanized.

In this connection the question arises as to whether the development of communism can be influenced or whether there is nothing to be done but to wait for the natural development to take its course. Various facts would seem to favor the latter attitude. First of all, the communist part of the world, after its expansion to a supranational order of magnitude, is passing through a grave crisis the outcome of which remains uncertain.

Communism presupposes great faith, but the communist world is morally riddled with dissension. The Soviet-Chinese schism (preceded by that of Yugoslavia and the Soviets), Trotskyist tendencies in some of the developing countries, the technological lag relative to the USA, and many other factors account for the relatively poor showing of the stock of communism on the international exchange. The hope for an international crisis of capitalism has largely come to be illusory, for capitalism in its present modified form, that is, through the embodiment in it of such socialist principles of economics as advance planning, is quite able to withstand and even to ward off severe crises. The regressive course of communism in the technologically highly developed countries of the West weakens the hope of the eastern block of strengthening its economic potential through the take-over of great industrial countries. It seems entirely possible that the rating of the ideological stock of communism will continue to decline. Is this going to signify that the Vatican will lose interest in it?

A minority group—with dwindling numbers of adherents—advocates nonintervention and noninterference on the ground of the claim that "communists cannot be argued with," for they are "dialectically indoctrinated." The first of these points implies that communists are not human beings but automata. A point to be considered in this connection is that the communists in non-communist countries are socially discriminated against, as the result of which they have maneuvered themselves into a petrified posture of defense. As for the matter of "dialectical indoctrination," all one can say is that it is a myth in about the same way as the rumors of the power and the secrets of the Jesuits are a myth.

How, now, can one exert an influence on the development of communism as a world movement? In countries in which the communists are in power they tend to be dogmatically stolid. Then, too, despite their dialectical training, they are afraid of the effectiveness of any kind of highly qualified non-communist literature. It is the communists who invented the concept of "coexistence," but they interpret it from case to case as they see fit. The response of the Second Vatican Council was the launching of the counterconcept of the "dialogue," which many ruling communist parties fear in precisely the same way as the conservative Catholics fear it. To be afraid of a dialogue is not exactly proof of one's inner strength.

In Christian quarters—occasionally also, in a totally naive way, in conservative circles in Soviet communism—the principle of the dialogue is at times attacked on the basis of the argument that Italian, French, or Austrian communists would utilize a "dialogue" for exclusively "tactical" purposes, that is, they would not have the slightest intention of letting their real position become the subject of questions and answers. If this argument contains a grain of truth, it certainly does not apply to more than a minority of the communists.

In the course of a discussion which an Austrian socialist had with a Soviet philosopher in Tiflis, the latter proved quite impervious to any attempt on the part of his interlocutor to establish the atmosphere of a serious dialogue. When he was confronted with quotations from the writings and public utterances of his "comrade" Togliatti, he tried to get out from under by the observation—infantile, to be sure, in an exchange with a noncommunist but doubtless adequate to restore his own dogmatic peace of mind—that "comrade Togliatti means that no doubt only tactically."

It is quite certain, on the other hand, that there are numerous communists who proceed frankly and honestly in their discussions. After all, the situation among the Catholics is in no way different. There are Catholics who are honestly ready for a dialogue and others to whom a dialogue is a "tactical maneuver."

It should be noted here that with respect to this problem of the "dialogue," the situation in Italy is considerably more favorable than it is, for instance, in the Federal Republic of Germany. The progressive open-mindedness of the West German clergy is a myth or at best a half-truth of limited applicability. At the Vatican Council, most of the West German bishops displayed a progressive attitude only in questions in which the attitudes of the Protestants are progressive. This suggests that the Catholic bishops had derived from their confrontation with the Protestants, that is, as a matter of historical experience, the conviction that Protestants are not necessarily tools in the hands of the devil.

The Italian bishops who have been similarly confronted with Italian communists, have arrived at similar convictions relative to communism and the communists. There are cases of blood relationship between high-ranking members of the Italian Catholic hierarchy and high-ranking functionaries of the Italian Communist Party. To be sure, the dogmatic communists of the eastern countries represent, from the Catholic point of view, a serious problem as a result of the fact that they have created a totally "fouled-up" political situation relative to the Church. On the other hand, the problem which honest communists in the West represent to the Catholics is no less serious, though it rather assumes the appearance of a challenge.

Speaking specifically of the communists in the western countries, a point to be stressed is that they live in a liberal environment in which they have seen fit to withdraw in one sense or another into a ghetto of their own creation without being able to plug their ears to all the arguments of their adversaries. It is for this reason that there is hardly an intellectual Italian or French communist whose thinking and speaking about theological problems reflects the same uninformed candor and schematic inflexibility that characterizes in this area the thinking and speaking of most Soviet communists whose "theological horizon" is normally somewhat restricted. In fact, from the point of view of the communists of the West, a dialogue with spokesmen of Catholicism is politically extremely advantageous, for it boosts in a sense the value of their stock in trade. There is also the fact that their social appeal, that is, their potential of expansion, is depleted. They would find it impossible to build up by themselves a communist state or even, in a less extreme sense, any state of Marxist or socialist orientation. To do so they would need allies.

It thus seems natural that they should turn to those whose class interests are congruent with socialism, whose moral principles are compatible with the socialist ideology, with the secondary qualification that they are no atheists, that is to say: the Christians. In addition, there are in the West many communists to whom the Stalinist crimes proved extremely sobering so that they are ready to prefer dialogue to terror. Not a few of

these speak openly in favor of cultural freedom, they label "socialist realism" stupid, consider the suppression of religion nonsense,
and regard the "leashing" of science as a grave and fundamental error. As a matter of genuine conviction and simultaneously in the interest of their party, they begin to criticize their
eastern comrades and do so to a large extent in terms indistin-
guishable from the Catholic approach. The result is that of a
sudden the communist parties in the east censure those in the
west. The Soviet Union, in particular, finds itself here in a difficult
position. A case in point is the fact that Luigi Longo's statements
at the 1966 convention of the Italian Communist Party were
censured in Moscow and withheld from publication. Such things
have a way of getting around. There is today in Moscow a group
whom the party-line faithful refer to as "Italians."

In the long run Moscow cannot afford to alienate the strongest
communist party of the West, that is, the Italian Communist
Party. The Kremlin has begun to go easy in the matter of its
own infallibility. The was out of this dilemma might be summed
up as follows: Every communist party is autonomous and may
proceed as it sees fit. If the Italians think they should enter into
an alliance with the Catholics, let them do so. Meanwhile the rest
of us will continue to back by administrative measures the idea
of the historical necessity of the gradual disappearance of all
religion.

In reality, however, things are not that simple, and Moscow
knows it. But it is by no means clear what can be done in this
situation. The Catholics in the West are not dumb enough to
make concessions to western communism without insisting on a
quid pro quo. Their arguments run somewhat like this: You go
and convince your eastern comrades that they must modify their
politics relative to the Church, that they must grant genuine
freedom of religion. Then come back, and we will be ready to talk
about other things, too.—This type of argument is not unlike
that presented by groups outside the Church in connection
with the Church's attitude in Spain. At the time of the Second
Vatican Council high-ranking members of the Spanish clergy
opposed the freedom of religion demanded by many of their
peers from other countries. They insisted that freedom of reli-

gion might be all right for certain countries, but not for Spain, where conditions were different. In their opinion, it was incumbent upon the Church to adjust its procedures in each individual country to the prevailing conditions. Obviously, such a demand weakens the credibility of the Catholic Church with respect to its readiness for tolerance. The same thing applies to communism too. The liberalism of western communists cannot be expected to be taken at face value until it is practiced in the east as well. On the basis of this kind of logic, numerous individual Catholic bishops strove to make their Spanish brethren see the light, and in doing so they became spokesmen of the non-Catholic world. In precisely the same way, many western communists recognize the soundness of the Catholic position and strive to make their eastern comrades see the light. This makes them the best-qualified emissaries of Christianity in the east.

All this makes clear that it is entirely possible to exert an influence on the development of communism. Indeed, it would be unwise to miss this chance.

It goes without saying that inversely the communists, too, can exert an influence on the development of Catholicism, for the Catholics are likewise far from deaf. Yet, a shift to the left within the Church cannot be promoted by overstressing the Marxist principle of "historical necessity," by locking up members of the clergy, by refusing to take part in the "dialogue," by closing houses of worship under the pretense that they are "structurally unsafe," by setting up atheist museums in which pendulums and neon lights are used to demonstrate the nonexistence of God, and—all in all—by being rabidly "progressive."

For any kind of rapprochement between Catholicism and communism, a point of particular importance is that the idea must be quashed that community ownership of the means of production and atheism go necessarily hand in hand.

The two are in no way causally interrelated. Christian socialism and even Christian communism are entirely conceivable. There is nothing in the Gospels that could be adduced as an argument against community ownership of the means of production. On the contrary, many Gospel passages speak in favor of such a system. One might cite the theses of St. Thomas More in his *Utopia* to prove that it is possible to combine theism and a socialist system of economics and societal organization. It may be foreseen that the ideas of Thomas More have a great future in the Church. He was canonized at just the right time, on the fifteenth of May, 1935, that is, the day and the month when encyclicals of social import are usually published.

The most recent social encyclical of Paul VI, *Populorum progressio,* represents—after the same Pope's appeal to Christian employers of 1964—an extraordinarily courageous act which came as a surprise, considering what we have come to expect from Paul VI.

The encyclical was, to say the least, extremely embarrassing to the conservative Christian democratic parties, whose leaders include not a few who cling to their childhood faith in a petit-bourgeois "Christian social doctrine" (of a home, a shop, and a nest egg for every family), though it is certainly true that many of these men would still fail to recognize the shift to the left of the Church, or rather, would still refuse to recognize that shift if an encyclical were to appear beginning with the words, "Proletarians of all countries, unite!"

When a socialist system declares that it makes no difference whether the principle of society ownership of the means of production is endorsed for theistic or for atheistic reasons, that system makes room for a philosophical and religious pluralism through which it becomes tolerant and liberal. Such a system would have a socialist "base" with a liberal "superstructure." In it the Church could pursue its objectives without touching the basis of the state.

Since in the eastern states the Communist Party is in power and no doubt will remain in power in the foreseeable future, it is not enough to pursue the "strategic" objective of a neutralization of the state with respect to religion. The state is an instrument of the party in power. It is hence the party that must assume a neutral position and tolerate not only religion-oriented members but also religion-oriented functionaries, as in fact the Communist Party of Italy already does. As a transitional phase, neutralization on a state basis seems entirely desirable. Communist functionaries would have to begin by displaying tolerance within the framework of their state functions and subsequently also within the party.

Such a development is quite in keeping with the inescapably foreseeable resolution of the conflict currently still prevailing between the educational policies of the communist states and their continued endeavor to prescribe to their intellectuals a diet of informational abstinence. This conflict cannot but be resolved in the long run in favor of the intellectuals, for the Soviet Union and the other eastern states pursue expansive educational policies not only for economic and, in fact, military reasons but are bound for ideological reasons to produce a great number of intellectuals. Now, it is a simple fact of nature that illiterates readily accept censorship of the press because they cannot read anyway. The response of the intellectual is bound to be the opposite. From a humanistic and humanitarian point of view it is, to be sure, a praiseworthy endeavor to disclose the world of knowledge to as many individuals as possible, but the procedure involves the disclosure of a world which brooks no limitation by the censorship of any kind of bureaucracy. The *Index librorum prohibitorum* of Rome had to be abandoned. Moscow will find that its "indexes" will also have to be abandoned. Tanks powerful enough to suppress this dynamic fact will never be built.

Finally, no communist party anywhere in the world will find it possible in the long run to prevent the development of a communist pluralism within its own ranks. If even with respect to a question such as that of the occupation of Czechoslovakia, the Soviet Communist Party has to put up with the fact that diverse points of view were represented in the response of world communism, with the implication that all those points of view could be regarded as communist, then it is rationally not possible in the long run to refuse to accept a similar pluralism within the framework of the home base, that is, the Soviet Russian Communist Party. If the viewpoint prevailingly represented with respect to a particular question within the Italian Communist Party is regarded as communistically sound, then it is impossible to deny that the same position is likewise communistically sound when it is upheld by a Soviet communist. This remains true, no matter how often the formula is reiterated

—a formula, by the way, which the communists of Czechoslovakia undertook to revise officially—that after a vote the minority must uphold the theses of the majority, which is clearly incompatible with the principles of the freedom of conscience.

Against such reflections there is no argument that deserves to be taken seriously, and there is also no reliable method permitting the prediction as to when we shall witness a definitive breakthrough to freedom of opinion and conscience inside the USSR. A Swiss newspaper summarized the situation with remarkable journalistic succinctness in the headline, "Waiting for Moscow's Dubcek." There is considerable evidence that this breakthrough will come fairly soon. In particular, the occupation of Czechoslovakia can be claimed to have accelerated the preparatory process in dialectical terms.

Meanwhile the Church is tactically concerned with maintaining the terrain won so far in the eastern states. If it can obtain on the part of its antagonists in this game an attitude of coolly detached friendliness, it can claim to have scored a distinct success, for this implies that it has gained time—time which is of the essence—for the realization of long-term plans.

To be sure, considering the political realities in the people's democracies, objectives of the kind here alluded to are bound to look, to say the least, utopian. But fifteen years ago, the situation as it is today would also have seemed unrealistic. The Vatican must plan its strategy with a view to the future. In the course of its bimillennial history the Church has learned to be patient.

Historical Particulars

The relationship of the Vatican with the "East" can be most readily characterized if one takes up the various components of it one at a time. The greatest importance in this connection is to be attributed to the relationship of the Vatican with the Kremlin as the center of communism. If one takes into consideration population-statistical information on the numbers of Catholics in the various countries, the relationship between the Church and Poland assumes increased significance. In the following passages historical facts will be adduced only by reason of the determining influence they may have exerted on the present eastern politics of the Vatican. In other words, the question will be: In what way have the events of the past affected the shape of things in the present and how can specific events of the present be explained on the basis of the past? The actions and reactions of Cardinal Wyszynski or of the patriarch Alexis cannot be understood exclusively in terms of the Christian faith. They must be viewed simultaneously as reflecting Polish and Russian experiences and insights throughout the centuries. And the communist actors, too, depend at least in part on the experiences and insights of their predecessors.

The Vatican and the Kremlin

The term "Kremlin" is in this connection a symbol of Russia. It represents a dynamic continuity older than and continuing beyond the Soviet revolution.

For European history—and hence for world history as well—it was extremely important, perhaps decisively so, that the Russians and Ukrainians did not accept the Christianity of Rome but the Christianity of Byzantium. A sound evaluation of this fact, particularly with respect to its implications for Catholicism, is by no means easy. For Christianity as a whole, and the Catholic world in particular, it may well prove to have been wholesome in the long run that the Church of Byzantium became linked to a powerful political center, permitting it to preserve the Christian truths which the Church of Rome in its imperialist struggle for power was bound to neglect. To be sure, a Catholic needs to have a highly developed sense of the dialectics of history to understand the thesis that in the final analysis the schism may prove to have been beneficial to his church.

It is entirely conceivable that already at the time of their conversion to Christianity the princes of Russia and the Ukraine regarded the struggle for power of the Roman Church as more ominous and dangerous than the missionary objectives of Byzantium, for Rome's striving for power was manifest not only in the continuity of the spiritual heritage of Constantine but also in Rome's emphasis on the principle of centralization. By comparison, the Orthodox Church appeared rather decentralized and hence politically less potent, less endowed with an effective striking potential.

The motive underlying the schism was precisely the motive underlying the decision of the eastern Slavs to turn to the Church of Byzantium. In the Orthodox liturgy Slavic came to be the Church language while the Roman Church continued for centuries to retain Latin. This fact played an important role in the tensions between Orthodox Eastern Europe and the Catholic West, although it must not be overlooked that political reasons came to be responsible for religious dissension within the Slavic world, too. The Poles and the Croats joined the Roman Church, with the result of dramatic conflicts between Poles and Russians and Croats and Serbs.

It goes without saying that since the time when the schism between Rome and Byzantium first began the Vatican has been striving to win back the Orthodox faithful, that is, to have them rejoin the Church of Rome. The fact as such and its ultimate motivation require no comment. It is the methods used in the pursuit of that objective and the type of reunion envisaged that can be subject to differences of opinion. Up to the time of the Russian revolution, the Vatican's eastern politics was mainly concerned with leading the Orthodox back into the "wide embrace" of the Church (Pius XII). Prior to the enthronement of John XXIII and the Second Vatican Council initiated by him, these endeavors were basically characterized by a kind of aggressive imperialism which it is impossible to understand except in the historical continuity of the seizure of power by the patrician families of Rome and the growing influence feudalism exerted on the Church.

Initially the Christianization of a whole people or its reunion with the Church of Rome was not seen as a problem involving the individual decision of each member of that people. It was simply the princes that were being Christianized or the bishops whose decision to rejoin Rome was sought. When this was accomplished, the whole people—which "most humbly" had to do what the God-willed authority ordered—was automatically Christianized or reunited with Rome. This conception of "rulers and subjects" dominated Vatican thinking up to the time of John XXIII. Cardinal Ruffini has not broken away from it even today. He cannot conceive of the relationship between bishops and laity in terms other than those of the relationship between officers and troops, which in the last analysis is akin to the relationship of masters and slaves. Orthodox and Catholic populations got thus to be united and reunited with no one bothering to as much as consult the "subjects" involved. The earliest exemplification of the procedure was the union within Greater Poland. The last was the reunion in the Ukraine accomplished in 1946 with the help of Stalin.

The missionary activity of the Orthodox Church in the east did not substantially differ from that of the Roman Church in the west. In the form of the new religion the aristocrats were offered a more effective ideology of rulership, and the subjects were baptized on a wholesale basis. The same principle applied in matters of union and reunion. Once the ruling princes were won over for the idea, their decision became binding for all their subjects.

But what happened when the princes failed to heed the will of the Church? When a ruling house died out, there was the possibility that a shift in the balance of power had to be coped with. Otherwise the most obvious procedure for the extension of power, from a feudalist point of view, was armed conquest.

Prior to the papacy of Pius XII, the Vatican thought of reunion exclusively in terms of submission, involving for the "faithless" deserters of the Mother Church that they would do penance and kiss the rod. The possibility that a secession might have been motivated by the desire to remain faithful to the truth was as inconceivable to feudal thinking as the possibility that "schismatics" and "heretics"—referred to as "separated brethren"—might possibly have derived from their endeavor to be faithful to the truth the qualification of preserving Christian values or possibly even of defending them against the Roman hybris. This implies that there was not the slightest inkling of an expectation that the reunification with the Orthodox Church might bring with it an enrichment of Catholicism. There was nothing reminiscent of a desire for a higher form of synthesis.

There was exclusively the notion that rebellious subjects had to be brought to heel.

Since the Orthodox princes gave no sign of being willing to submit to the Vatican, the Roman Church had only two possibilities of working toward an integration. The attempt could be made to convince the princes by arguments or the princes could be excluded. To be sure, when there was no possibility of excluding the princes, arguments had to be relied upon, but when the possibility of getting rid of the princes presented itself, what reason was there not to make use of that possibility?

Russia, like Byzantium, was to be conquered. The faithless subjects were to be forced back into submission. The Pope himself had only insignificant armed forces at his disposal, but he could make use of the orders of knights whose main mission, after all, was "to fight the infidels." In terms of brutality there was little to give one of these orders the edge over the others, though in the fights against the Slavs and the Baltic peoples it was particularly the Teutonic Order that distinguished itself. In the Near East, the Knights of the Cross were fighting against the heathens. It was particularly the Fourth Crusade—which led in 1204 to the conquest of Byzantium—that represented a severe blow to the Orthodox Church.

The Teutonic Knights in their state did not always toe the line of the directives given them by the Popes. It was understood, for instance, that they would treat those of their subjects who had accepted baptism differently from those who had not. This induced the Knights in many cases to prevent the baptism of their new subjects for reasons arising from their class interests; that is to say, their behavior was comparable to that of Mohammedan slave owners who did not convert their slaves to Mohammedanism because this would have implied that they had to be set free. Furthermore, the Knights tried to conquer Catholic Poland because, in their view, Poland was not as yet "as Catholic as it ought to be." The attempt of the Teutonic Order to conquer Russia wound up in failure. In two great battles, Alexander Nevski defeated first the Swedes on the banks of the Neva (1240) —hence the honorific Nevski—and then the Teutonic Order on the ice of Lake Peipus (1242). In Russia Alexander Nevski is not only honored as a national hero but he is also revered as a saint because he saved his country from foreign rule and his Church from being subjugated by Roman aggression. This explains why inside the Soviet Union the news was received with considerable satisfaction that the Vatican was giving serious consideration to the possibility of granting Alexander Nevski the status of a saint also in the Roman Catholic Church.

Such a politically skillful move on the part of Rome would signify that the Vatican has definitively decided to close the chapter of its feudal power politics against the Russians and also that it has dissociated itself from the historical German Eastern politics, the continuity of which appears in a new perspective when we realize that the National Socialists revived in fact the politics of conquest of the Teutonic Order. Alexander Nevski did not succeed in destroying the state of the Teutonic Order, this blot on the shield of honor of Christianity. As a result we were not spared the development of the Prussian military mentality of command and obedience first cultivated in and by the Order of Teutonic Knights.

While the struggle against the Teutonic Order was going on, the Tatars of Genghis Khan invaded Russia. In 1240 Kiev fell into their hands. The Russians resisted stubbornly, and the Tatars had to conquer each individual town. This signifies that the Russians did a great deal for the Christian West, provided one shares the opinion that the yoke of the Tatars was unbearable. That this opinion is not necessarily the only one possible becomes clear when we recall that the Tatars respected freedom of religion and conscience. A great many Christians hailed their arrival because it freed them from the Islamic yoke, though here again the Tatars no doubt exploited the situation as they saw it.

In Rome the idea was seriously advanced—and it was by no means an illusory idea—that the Tatars might be won over to Christianity and be made an integral part of the West, with the collateral that the eastern Slavs would be led back into the Roman Church. This plan of procedure reflects practical Vatican politics. Michael de Fernandy[11] goes so far as to suggest that the reason the Occident did not come to the rescue of the beleagured Hungarians may well have been that—while the subjugation of

Hungary had to be taken for granted—there was the hope that it would be possible to come to an agreement with the Mongols. This may be an oversimplification, but the basic idea of winning over the Tatars was by no means as wild as it might seem at first blush. Eduard Winter wrote in this connection:

An offer in this sense made to the Tatars by the Popes was not at all unrealistic. At the Court of the Great Khan there were influential circles belonging to Nestorian Christianity. The decision as to which world religion the Tatars would ultimately embrace was still open at the time. It goes without saying that the Tatars were not guided in their choice of a religion by religious considerations. What interested them were questions of power politics. They were concerned with having the world religion they embraced facilitate their world conquest or—once it was accomplished—consolidate it in its inner structure. Since, on the other hand, the Popes were interested in establishing their spiritual world rule at any price, a meeting of the minds (and ways) of the two powers was in the last analysis by no means a far-fetched proposition. To be sure, considering the claim of the Popes to be recognized as "emperors of emperors" and the consciousness of the Tatar Khans that they were destined to a position of universal power, an alliance of the two powers could not but prove to be utopian. However, this could not be clear without a meeting and an encounter.[12]

In fact, the game the Vatican was trying to play at this juncture was a repetition of its maneuvers at the time of the Frankish kings. From the point of view of Rome and Greece, Pepin the Short or, for that matter, Charlemagne, was no less of a barbarian than Genghis Khan was from the point of view of the entire Occident. The emperor of Byzantium was considered the protector of the Church, but he proved too weak to force the Orthodox into submission, and so Rome placed its hope in the robust barbarians in the North, that is to say, the Teutons. The uncouth savagery of those creatures could easily be forgotten in view of the fact that they were strong. In a similar way, the fact that Genghis Khan was a barbarian was not particularly important from Rome's point of view. One has to admit in this connection that the Vatican has never had any kind of sympathy with any kind of racism. Slit eyes and bow legs cut no ice in the thinking of the Vatican. If the Pope had assumed toward the Mongols the same attitude of humility which his predecessor displayed toward Pepin and Charlemagne, it is quite conceivable that with the help of the Mongols the Russians could have been forced to agree to a union with Rome or even to submit to complete Latinization.

The following anecdote may seem but arduously related to our subject, but the evaluation of the politics of the Vatican by a "Christian-democratic" politician is indirectly both interesting and illuminating.

When Konrad Adenauer was in Vienna he was taken, among other things, to the treasure chamber in the Hofburg. His hosts expected that Adenauer, confronted with the Crown of the Holy Roman Empire—which after all has often enough and long enough been on the heads of German princes—would in one sense or another be "moved," that somehow a hidden German pride would be manifest in his response. To the great amazement of the Austrian members of his party nothing of the sort occurred. In deprecating appreciation Adenauer remarked: "In a way, you know, what the Pope was up to at that time was really a mean trick. After all, the real Christian emperor was in Byzantium. The poor fellow got double-crossed."

It appears that Adenauer somehow identified himself with the Byzantine emperor in opposition to the Franks. In him the Christian politician outranked the German politician.

Is it possible that he foresaw the fate of his own politics? In the end the Vatican "dropped" him in favor of the communist "east," in much the same way in which it had dropped the emperor in Byzantium in favor of the Germanic barbarians. As a matter of fact, it sometimes seems that the Vatican has a predilection for barbarians, for the barbarians of today may well represent the forces to which the future belongs.

But let us return to the Tatars and Russians.

Simultaneously the Vatican undertook the attempt to enter into an alliance with the Russians against the Mongol Khans, suggesting that the Russians pay for the help they might get from the Vatican in their fight against the Mongols by agreeing to come into the Catholic fold. The simultaneous adoption of both lines proved in the end to be self-defeating hyperdiplomacy. The

Russians decided that the Tatar yoke was preferable to waging
an uncertain war of liberation with the uncertain help proffered
by the Vatican.

After the failure of all plans to have the Russians "come
home" either with the help of the Tatars or in payment for
help against the Tatars, other means had to be found to accomplish that objective. The relevant plants called successively for
the enlistment of help from the Northern States, the Orders of
Knighthood, Hungary, then the Lithuanians, the Poles, and
finally the Lithuanian-Polish empire that was to effect the catholicization of Russia. Indeed, the union of Lithuania and Poland
by marriage resulted in the establishment of a major power complex. The facts and events summarized in the following para-
graphs have been analyzed in considerable detail by Eduard
Winter.[13]

The Lithuanians and Poles attacked Russia at a time when it
still suffered under the Tatar yoke. This came to the Russians
as a particularly bitter blow. In the summer of 1610 a Polish
army reached Moscow. Treason enabled the Poles to get inside
the Kremlin and to take Moscow. In 1611 the Muscovites re-
belled, but the Poles were able to suppress the uprising. However, in 1612—that is, only one year later—Russian troops
coming down from the North re-entered the Kremlin. The Polish
power of expansion seemed to have spent itself. The patriarch of
Moscow, Hermogen, who steadfastly refused to crown the Polish
king, starved to death in prison. He is still being celebrated—and
rightly so—"as a true pastor and teacher," who "defended his
flock like a lion against wolves and robbers." [14] Another attempt
on the part of the Poles to conquer Moscow collapsed outside
the walls of the city. Slowly the Russians got ready to strike back.

Within the empire of Greater Poland, which remained strong
and powerful for a long time to come, the problem of the Orthodox integration was of special significance. The differences in
faith between the predominantly Roman Catholic inhabitants
of the original territory of the Lithuanian-Polish state and the
Orthodox population of the conquered areas raised a number of
questions the solution of which was an urgent desideratum not
only in terms of the national interest but also in terms of the ad-

ministrative practice of day-to-day rule. The Polish kings would doubtless have found a religiously homogeneous population more desirable.

These aspects of the problem concerned the Vatican only indirectly. The Vatican's interest in Poland was restricted to the matter of the country's Catholicism. The main point was the objective of winning over the Orthodox portions of the population. A unified Church in Poland promised to convince the Orthodox within the Russian state structure that it would be no disadvantage for the Eastern Church to be subject to the Pope. This implied of course that that Church must be given the possibility of a free development and that its forced Latinization would be avoided. These considerations resulted in a conflict of interest still manifest in the attitude of Cardinal Wyszynski toward the Vatican. In those early days, the Vatican held the Orthodox and their liturgy in contempt, for the "true" faith was the Latin Roman form, but this attitude was generally restrained in deference to the basic interest of the Vatican. This was concerned with winning over the Orthodox. The means was the united, that is, the Uniat, Church. Among the Orthodox this speculation met with distaste, manifest in their aggressive attitude toward the Uniats, which was in fact more belligerent than their attitude toward the Roman Catholic Church. A marked change in this situation occurred only during the Second Vatican Council.

In the Uniat Church the authority of the Pope was accepted, but the priests were not held to the principle of celibacy, and the Orthodox liturgy as well as the Orthodox church organization was retained. The Polish kings thought of the Uniat Church as merely a phase of transition that was to be followed by complete Latinization. The union had been accomplished under conditions the legitimacy of which was doubted by the Russians. The prevailing political situation—permitting an influence of the Polish State on the election of bishops and the like—lend credence to that doubt. Obviously, the union did not satisfy all priests nor all the faithful, and many persisted in their unqualified Orthodoxy despite the substantial disadvantages which this attitude entailed. It should be noted that the Polish insistence on Latinization did result in similar disadvantages also for the Orthodox who had accepted the union.

It was primarily thanks to the efforts of the bishop of Vitebsk and Tolotsk, Josaphat Kuncevicz, that the union was accomplished. The methods he used to achieve his goal were not always spiritual in their orientation. They not only seem incompatible with the definitions of the freedom of conscience and faith promulgated during the Second Vatican Council, they were not even in keeping with the theses of St. Thomas Aquinas. He did not hesitate to have Orthodox houses of prayer demolished and members of the Orthodox clergy thrown in prison. In the fall of 1623 there was an uprising in the course of which Josaphat was murdered. For the Uniat Church he had thus become a martyr and was subsequently canonized. The Orthodox regarded him as a symbol of the expansion of the Catholic Church and of the suppression of Orthodoxy.

Archbishop Josaphat was a Ukrainian. Another martyr of the united Church in the Ukraine, the Jesuit Andreas Bobola, was a Pole. He was killed by Cossacks for his stubborn resistance to an independent Ukraine.[15]

Conservative Poles harbor against Josaphat—by reason of his Ukrainian descent (which, in their eyes, is a flaw in any man's character)—a certain antipathy, which in its ultimate motivation may well be related to what induced the conservative bishops of Poland during the Second Vatican Council to keep aloof in the matter of the objections raised by the Ukrainians in exile against the presence of Russian Orthodox observers. Conservative Russians, too, despise the Ukrainians and display considerable reserve in their feelings toward the active Ukrainian renegade Josaphat.

In the tug of war between the Roman Catholic and the Orthodox Churches, St. Josaphat—represented by his bones—continued to play a peculiar role. During the First World War his relics were taken from Lwów to Vienna, the capital of the last remaining Catholic state, to protect them from the advancing Russian troops. They were laid to rest in the Church of St. Barbara, the house of worship of the Uniat Ukrainians in Vienna.

During the Second World War, when Soviet troops reached Vienna, Catholic circles were understandably worried lest the Soviets might take the relics of the great enemy of Orthodoxy back to the Soviet Union. For this reason Josaphat's coffin was first taken to the crypt of the Cathedral of St. Stephen. Cardinal Innitzer turned for help to the United States Army chaplain Roman J. Nuwer, suggesting that the relics be removed from the Russian sphere of influence. Disguised as coal delivery men, Nuwer and a group of like-minded companions removed the coffin from the crypt, hid it under a truckload of coal, and took it to the American sector of Vienna. He subsequently had it flown in an American military plane to Rome.[16] After some delay Josaphat was entombed in St. Peter's. One should think that the Vatican returned the bones to Vienna when the danger had passed. Nothing of the sort. They stayed in Rome. What happened to them subsequently is a matter of interest in a later context.

When the Poles tried to go beyond the terms of the union and effect Latinization of the Orthodox, Pope Urban VIII decreed that the switch to another rite required an explicit act of papal dispensation and saw to it that such dispensations were forthcoming on rare occasions only. The Polish king Sigismund III voiced his astonishment in this matter, stating that one could not possibly wish to prevent anyone from following "the more certain and better rite." The whole high-handed contempt of the "Romans" and "Latins" for the Orthodox and the Uniats is manifest in this formulation.

Within the framework of Polish imperialism, Latin as the language of the Church had a function which it discharged otherwise only within the immediate reach of Rome, that is, it was uilized to homogenize the population, implying its Polonization, This may account for the stubborn resistance of conservative Polish bishops against the liturgical decisions of the Second Vatican Council. They did not want a liturgy in the Polish vernacular. Against this background one also understands the interest of Russian Orthodox dignitaries in the introduction of a Polish liturgy. Such a development would deprive Polish imperialism of a powerful instrument.[17]

The inner dissension with which Greater Poland was beset favored a slow, relentless advance of the Russians. After a Cossack uprising, the Ukraine fell to Russia, resulting in another war between Russia and Poland. In 1655 the Protestant Swedes invaded Poland, conquering virtually all of it within a short space of time. The most important fortified locality still in Polish possession was Czestochowa. In dire straits the Poles promised to proclaim the Virgin Mary Queen of Poland if the Swedes were to lift the siege. This is what the Swedes did, and so Mary became "Queen of Poland" and Czestochowa became an important place of pilgrimage. The King of Poland who had fled to the Austrian portions of Silesia performed the dedication ceremonies. This episode, which at first blush may seem to be of merely anecdotal interest, is important for the understanding of the mysticism of Cardinal Wyszynski.

In the territories reconquered by the Russians, the union was rescinded. This process, in which the Russians did not display extraordinary delicacy either, was finally completed in 1946 when under Stalin and the Patriarch of Moscow the last remnants of the Uniat Church in the Ukraine were liquidated. During the German occupation (1942) the Ukrainian bishops tried to proclaim an "independent" Ukraine under the patronage of Hitler. For this they were locked up by the Gestapo. After the reconquest of the Ukraine by the Russians, the bishops—insofar as the Russians could get hold of them—were sent to Siberia or liquidated. (In Lwów there were four bishops representing four different creeds.) Some Ukrainian bishops managed to reach Rome. The last of these was the metropolitan Slipyi whom Khrushchev had released from prison.

The Vatican naturally followed the rise of Russia and the decline of Polish power with great interest. It recognized that it would no longer be possible to conquer Russia—at least not with the help of the Poles. As a result, Poland as a factor in the expansion of Catholicism was written off, and the various partitions of Poland were not objected to by the Vatican.

With all the realism characteristic of Rome's patrician families, the Vatican now sought other means to achieve the Catholicization of Russia. Efforts were made to secure the good will of the czar. This naturally did not please the Polish kings, for if a czar had in fact given his agreement to the Union, he would, as it were, have become legitimized as a Catholic ruler. For this reason the Polish kings did their best to thwart the relevant efforts of the Pope. On one occasion, in fact, a papal legate was locked up in Poland for a year to prevent him from reaching St. Petersburg. Despite the distrust of the czars, the Vatican diplomats scored occasional successes, but these were never decisive in their implications.

In Vienna, the Pope's efforts to come to an understanding with the czar did not arouse unqualified enthusiasm either. In the interest of Austria-Hungary, Metternich wished for relations between the Vatican and the czar that were good enough to make negotiations possible but also bad enough to require his, Metternich's, services as a go-between. The concern lest the Pope might come to an understanding with the czar at the expense of Poland was by no means unfounded. Even after the partition of Poland that country was a major liability for Russia because the possibility of a revolution there could never be entirely discounted. The Popes kept hoping that the Catholic Poles would heed the papal admonition that they should submit to the "legitimate authority" of the czars. The Poles, however, were of a different mind. Only the high clergy heeded the papal admonitions. The lower clergy tended to side with the people.

The tendency to establish a Greater Poland did not disappear either. After the First World War Marshal Pilsudski tried once again to conquer the Ukraine, justifying his attempt on the basis of the thesis that the "natural frontiers" of Poland were the Baltic and the Black Sea.

Since in the nineteenth century the papacy was next to the czars the most reactionary power in Europe, a mutual rapprochement of the two seemed altogether natural. The Popes clamored for a restoration of the old pontifical state, and in this they needed the help of the czars. The czars, on the other hand, were aware of the revolutionary forces that were threatening their throne. That in the end the authority of the Popes proved unable to allay this threat is another matter.

The Orthodox Church in Russia was by no means more tolerant than the Catholic Church in other countries. It discriminated against the Catholics, with the result that these welcomed the revolution of 1917. The Bolsheviks regarded the Orthodox Church as the most powerful ideological bulwark of czarism and hence fought that Church along with all the other faiths, though —to be sure—at various times with varying degrees of intensity. The Soviet constitution does guarantee "freedom of conscience," signifying that the atheists have the "freedom of antireligious propaganda," while the Churches are granted "freedom of worship," but the underlying principle of "equality under the constitution" is no more than a paper reality. The Russians have never been known to be liberal, and the principle of fairness is alien to them. In this they greatly resemble the Church authorities. The way in which these latter have been ruling their "subjects" (whose status of creatures created in the "image of God" did not exempt them, for instance, from the practices of the "Holy Office") has never reflected much respect for the opinions and the free will of others (with the principle of "Christian love" or "Christian charity" being relegated far and farther into the background). The concept of a fair discussion is on the whole as hard to make clear to a Bolshevik as it is to a Cardinal of the Roman Curia.

To be sure, the establishment of the Soviet regime with its atheistically oriented ideological superstructure represented a severe blow to Catholicism. But the response of the Popes on this score has by no means been consistent and uniform. In fact, from time to time Rome derived from the situation the hope that a union with the Orthodox Church of Russia was now a more realistic project.

Benedict XV, who occupied the papal throne at the time of the October Revolution, tried hard to establish contact with the Bolsheviks. During the famine brought about in the Soviet Union in 1921 through Stalin's wild collectivization of agriculture, the Pope organized a relief program of major proportions.

In 1922, Cardinal Ratti succeeded Benedict as Pius XI. He continued the efforts of his predecessor on the same grand scale. During his pontificate the world witnessed the then sensational event of representatives of the Vatican and the Soviets taking up contact during the international conference at Genoa. This conference began on February 10, that is, just a few days after the enthronement of Pius XI on February 6, 1922.

On the day of the opening of the conference, Cardinal Gasparri declared:

"The ultimate principles of the Church imply no objection on its part against a communist form of government. In matters of economics the Church is agnostic. Its spiritual interests have nothing to do with matters of economic organization, and their pursuit is hence not bound to a particular social climate. The Church merely demands that the organization of the state, of whatever nature it may be, must not interfere with the freedom of religious worship, nor with the freedom of the priests to discharge the functions of their office." [18]

This signifies that the Church at that early time offered to drop its moderately capitalist social doctrine in favor of a communist natural law. To be sure, the communists with their excessively one-sided religious sociology were unable to understand this point. Many of them have not learned better even now.

At a dinner during the conference the Soviet Foreign Commissar Chicherin and the Special Representative of the Pope, Archbishop Sincero, were seen in conversation, and members of the Soviet and Vatican delegations exchanged visits.

Of course, the importance of these first contacts should not be overrated. But they should not be underrated, either. It was a matter of three steps ahead and two steps back.

Ultimately the negotiations of the Vatican and the Soviets that were thus initiated wound up in failure, but there remained—one might say as a sediment—a certain subconscious awareness of future possibilities in Soviet thinking in the area of foreign affairs. The progressively more savage persecution of the Church in the Soviet Union did make further contacts progressively more difficult.

As a result there was the well-remembered encyclical *Divini redemptoris* issued by Pius XII on March 18, 1937. The intransigence of Soviet politics was no doubt a contributing factor in the Vatican's conclusion that it could not but lend its support to fascism. It is no exaggeration to claim that Cardinal Pacelli, the later Pius XII, helped Hilter in 1933 to seize total power when he induced the Catholic Center Party to support Hitler's Enabling Act (and thus to sign its own death warrant).

All in all, then, the early contracts between the Vatican and the Soviets were at best an interlude, and Catholicism continued to regard communism and its Russian stronghold as traps laid by Satan. Pius XII was a late-feudal pope with—in the deepest recesses of his heart—racist sympathies. It was his hope—at least initially—that Hitler's armies would open the way for German missionaries and that the crushed Bolshevik empire would be Catholicized. The authoritarian orientation of the hierarchy of the Church—essentially the characteristic remnant of late feudalism—has an inner affinity with all the various secondarily feudalistic forms of fascism. In this light the notion of the Pope just referred to becomes understandable although it still remains a fact that that notion was a political blunder of the first magnitude. To round out the picture of Pius's mistaken evaluation of the political situation we need but remember the well-turned phrases he made use of to sanction, in further pursuit of his objective, the subjugation of Poland. Indeed, there could be no turn for the better as long as Pius XII and/or Stalin were alive.

In this as in so many other respects, John XXIII marked a decisive turn. Relative to the Soviet Union the attitude of the Vatican underwent a two-fold revision: On the one hand in matters involving Russian Orthodoxy and secondly in matters involving the communist government.

It would be naive to refuse to see that the Russian Church occupies a definite place in Soviet planning in the area of foreign affairs. Indeed, the Russian Church has been functioning more or less successfully in this sense, if only in order to bolster its position in terms of Russian domestic politics. At the present time the situation of the Russian Church is quite precarious. This is strikingly apparent from a complaint which two Russian Orthodox priests filed on December 15, 1965, with the Chairman of the Presidium of the Supreme Soviet relative to the unconstitutional intervention of the state in matters involving the principles of freedom of religion and conscience. Social pressure on the faithful is extremely strong, and it appears that the authorities do not even feel obliged to abide formally by the principles laid down in the constitution. To be sure, this situation may sooner or later undergo a fundamental change, and it is senseful to try to promote and accelerate such a change. Evidently, whatever is undertaken in this direction, the immediate reaction of the Soviet government must be carefully taken into consideration.

It is difficult to understand the eastern politics of the Vatican without some awareness of the political organization at the Papal See. The Department of State or Ministry of Foreign Affairs of the Vatican is the office of the Cardinal Secretary of State. This office normally functions with two undersecretaries of state. Pius XII was a passionate diplomat without any kind of pastoral experience, which explains his decision to take personal charge of the Secretariate of State. He acted in this like a head of government who acts as his own foreign minister. Pius XII appointed Cardinals Tardini and Montini as his undersecretaries of state, of whom the last-named subsequently became Pope as Paul VI. John XXIII again appointed a separate Cardinal Secretary of State. This was Cardinal Cicognani. The most important man in the eastern division came to be Monsignore Agostino Casaroli.

Just as in any other state it is not only the foreign ministry that is interested in foreign affairs and international politics, in the Vatican, too, various other institutions play an important role in this area, such as for instance the "Secretariate for Christian Unity." The former Holy Office under Cardinal Ottaviani with competency in matters involving the "purity of the faith" felt called upon by implication to supervise as it were the Vatican's demeanor in foreign affairs in ideological terms. There were in these various agencies men whose conservatism made them consider Monsignore Casaroli a "traitor" by reason of what he did in his eastern division of the Secretariate of State. Still another institution linked to the Vatican must be mentioned in this context, although it exerts no direct influence in political matters. This is the *collegium russicum* which is located near the church of Santa Maria Maggiore. Here members of the clergy are being trained in matters pertaining to the Soviet Union, and the teaching staff are clergymen who are specialists in this area. Among the professors are men like Gustav A. Wetter, S.J.,

Pietro Modesto, and Huber, S.J. They all are members of the Russian Uniat Church and therefore have beards, while the Russian Orthodox in the reunited areas of the Soviet Union are beardless. To be sure, most of these members of the Uniat Church were originally Roman Catholics who accepted the Russian Uniat rite at a later time in their lives. This holds true, for instance, for Professor Wetter.

At the *collegium russicum,* it goes without saying, the subjects taught include the history of the Russian Church. In the matter of the Polish-Russian conflict, this instruction is clearly slanted in favor of the Russians. The clerics who have completed their training at the *collegium* speak Russian and Old Slavic. They are able to function as interpreters. There are several hundreds of them.

It is of interest, however, that the Secretariate of State as well as the Secretariate for Christian Unity do not like to fall back on the *collegium russicum.* The diplomats feel they do not need the *collegium,* and the Secretariate for Christian Unity found itself until recently confronted with the difficulty that the Orthodox demanded the dissolution of the Uniat Churches as a minimum requirement without which they were not even ready to begin a dialogue. This situation, it is true, has greatly changed.

John XXIII wanted love in lieu of rule. He wanted peace, agreement, encounters of equals. This applied to the Bolsheviks as well as to the Orthodox. There were the beginnings of a rapprochement with the Bolsheviks as witness—as a first manifestation—the visit which John XXIII received from Adzhubei. Later on Paul VI was visited by Gromyko and Podgorny. John XXIII had a particular interest in the Orthodox since he had held the post of papal nuncio in Bulgaria and the Near East. During his pontificate he organized one of the most successful and valuable institutions at the Vatican: The Secretariate for Christian Unity, which he placed under the direction of Cardinal Bea. The Second Vatican Council, convened by John XXIII, was thought of as ecumenically oriented, implying specifically also the objective of a rapprochement with the "separated brethren," which was the new term for "schismatics" and "heretics."

By contrast to the First Vatican Council, various non-Roman Catholic churches—initially in particular Protestant churches—accepted the invitation to send observers. From the very beginning, these observers did not merely function as such but intervened effectively and emphatically in what was happening at the Council. To be sure, their presence was due to a very large extent to the confidence-inspiring personalities of John XXIII and Cardinal Bea. The Catholics and Orthodox have much more in common and are separated by fewer dogmatic differences than either or both and the Protestants. It is for this reason that it was particularly important that the orthodox should be represented at the Council by official observers.

Among the Orthodox the Patriarch of Constantinople, Athenagoras, is probably the most pro-Catholic. At the Conference of Rhodos he favored the appointment of observers at the Council. However, other Orthodox groups, especially those representing the extremely reactionary Greek Church, opposed this move, and Athenagoras finally accepted the majority decision—doubtless promoted by the Russian, too—that no observers should be sent. In terms of the ultimate intentions of John XXIII this matter was extremely important. It would have been a catastrophe for the Council as a whole if no single Orthodox Church had sent its observers. That was the great chance for the Russians (and for the communists). In short order it was learned that not only Polish bishops would make the trip to the Council but also bishops from Czechoslovakia, Hungary, East Germany, and Lithuania. Everything seemed beautifully arranged. And then followed the great sensation: Two observers of the Russian Church appeared in Rome and were given a friendly welcome. They were observers sent by a church of which rumor had it that its bishops were atheists. What had happened?

Among the Orthodox, the Patriarchate of Constantinople, previously Byzantium, is regarded as outstandingly venerable and sublime, for it is very old. Conservative souls tremble with emotion when they come face to face with a tradition that is old. By comparison, the Patriarchate of Moscow and of all of Russia is relatively young. Gauged by the standard of Byzantium it is a mere upstart. Nonetheless, in terms of numbers, it represents many more faithful (in the order of from 50 to 70 million) than Constantinople whose flock is numerically not particularly impressive. Ceremonies and the bestowal of meaningless honors are a specialty of Rome, and the Patriarch Athenagoras of Constantinople is of course being treated with the utmost respect, but the difference between form and substance is never lost sight of. It goes without saying that Rome attributes greater importance to Moscow than to Constantinople. Still, a pro-Caholic attitude on the part of the Patriarch of Constantinople is nothing to be sneezed at. After all, the influence of Patriarch Athenagoras within the Orthodox domain is not restricted to the circumscribed area technically assigned to him. The situation, as seen from the point of view of Rome, makes it possible to use the Russians to exert pressure on the Greeks and Athenagoras to sway the Russians. It is expedient to concentrate on the weakest spot.

As soon as the Russians showed signs that they were ready to stand apart from the Orthodox phalanx, they suddenly assumed great importance in Rome's thinking. The price of alienating Athenagoras—if this had seemed necessary—would not have been regarded as too high. Ultimately, however, the Russian initiative did not run counter to the endeavors of Athenagoras. For the moment, it is true, the Russians had stolen the show, but Athenagoras was able to make up for this when he and Paul VI met in Jerusalem and, before that, through the revocation of the mutual excommunication of Rome and Byzantium.

Today it is no longer possible to be of two minds in the matter of who was more interested in having observers at Rome: The Russian Orthodox Church of the Soviet Government. Khrushchev had promoted the decision with considerable energy. It is also to be noted that in the course of the Council the initially rather reserved attitude of the Russians underwent a striking change. Indeed, it became quite apparent that "being in touch" was a matter of interest not only from the point of view of the Vatican but also from that of the Soviet Union.

In this context, particular interest attaches to the observations of Max Lackmann, an open-minded German Lutheran, who—nonetheless—appears to be in this matter completely under the

spell of the political naivete of the Christian Democratic Union.
He wrote:

Anyone aware of the multifariousness and complexity of the patterns
of endeavor of the churches represented in the World Church Council
(or—if you will—in the more restricted domain of German Protestantism), anyone willing and able to evaluate fairly the forces that are
alive and rivaling one another in this area—they range from far to the
"left" to far to the "right"—would have wished that an attempt had
been made to establish contacts and to exchange information on a
broader basis of negotiation and discussion. It is to be feared that in the
situation as it came to be, important aspects of both the current state
of affairs and the hoped-for future of non-Catholic groups were never
touched upon and played no role in the final outcome. This applies in
particular to the Greeks who, in many respects, have reason to be
extremely sensitive. I am quite certain that I am not alone either here
in Rome or in Germany in having the impression that certain shunting
maneuvers and decisions of the Secretariate—exemplified in a climactic
way by the trip to Moscow undertaken toward the end of September
on the initiative of Archbishop Nikodim by Monsignore Willebrands—
were governed more centralistically than one would have liked (and
in using the term "centralistic" I am thinking less of Rome than of
Geneva). It is no secret to what extent the Roman Curia and its theologians lack a thoroughgoing appreciation of the need to discard certain concepts which I do not hesitate to call "un-Catholic" and which
until now have made it impossible for many members of the Greek
Orthodox Church to believe—Pope John and his Cardinal Bea to the
contrary notwithstanding—that Rome has shifted its position relative
to the Orthodox tradition and the culture of the east to deserve to be
called truly "Catholic."

So far Lackmann is certainly right. But then he went on to ask
the decisive question:

What was it that induced Rome so suddenly—after Patriarch Athenagoras had been so outspoken in voicing his sympathies for John
XXIII and the restoration of unity with Rome—to take up negotiations
with Moscow without the participation of Athenagoras—in a certain
sense even against Athenagoras—that is to say, negotiations with a
church that had agreed to send observers to the Council only under
certain conditions of which it is by no means certain that they are

acceptable as a matter of principle from the point of view of a Council of the Church of Jesus Christ? (It will be remembered that at the World Church Conference in New Delhi the presence of the Russian delegates raised the same problem with respect to the conditions in the Eastern Zone of Germany.) . . . What price is the Catholic Church willing to pay for the presence of observers representing the Patriarchate of Moscow? Is the Catholic Church aware of the price that has already been paid in the World Church Council by the admission of Russian Orthodoxy? Whose diplomacy won out in this game, and who will have to foot the bill? [19]

These questions can only be answered by one who has understood the new basic attitude of Pope John XXIII, and that—obviously—is a thing which Max Lackmann does not understand. He noticed (and understood) that John XXIII had begun to be pleasant, amiable, and—in a word—very nice to the Protestants, and that pleased Lackmann. But really, a Pope should know better than to display that same attitude toward the communists. That sort of thing should be reserved for the progressive wing of the Christian Democratic Union. This is the level of Lackmann's critical appreciation when he writes:

It might not be a bad idea for the Catholic ecumenicists in Rome to lend more than half an ear to their troublesome mentor in the Holy Office who remains dead set against the coexistence of Church and communism. [20]

Lackmann was annoyed to find that it was initially only the Russian Orthodox that came to Rome. And he was quite right when he noted critically:

But Rome could have done considerably more in the course of the precious years of the immediate past to prove to the distrustful Orthodox (whose distrust is not necessarily unfounded) that it is their independent existence, their theology, their Catholic contribution and not exclusively their "return" and their "submission" that is deemed worthy of interest. But little happened along these lines. "You know," I was told by a churchman who had been living in Athens, "the Greeks do have a way of saying mean things about the Roman Catholic Church." Surely the Greeks, too, have a share in the responsibility for the failure. And indeed, critical voices begin to be heard in their own camp. The well-known Greek-Orthodox theologian, Professor Alivisatos qualified the decision of the Patriarchate of Constantinople and of the Greek Church to send no observer to the Second Vatican Council as "an excusable historical error in judgment." And he continued: "So here we are now—all alone—in the enjoyment of our orthodoxy and our ecumenicity and let the press inform us about what is going on in Rome, while other churches doubtless occupy our legitimate place." [21]

It is not surprising that the presence of the Russians in Rome did not meet with everybody's approval. The Christian love of many a Council Father was put to a hard test. Particularly the Ukrainian bishops, who could not forget the year 1945, felt overtaxed when they were expected to act and react in the spirit of John XXIII. Lackmann began his report with the description of a press conference:

At the beginning of the conference Monsignore Willebrands, as the head of the Secretariate for Christian Unity, read in French a prepared statement which made quite a stir. It cast a special light on certain events of the last few days which had come as a shock to many, although Catholic circles—doubtless out of deference to individual personalities —strove to have them played down in the press. Monsignore Willebrands' statement follows: "The Secretariate for the Advancement of Christian Unity wishes to stress that all observer-delegates are guests of the Secretariate and should feel that the welcome extended to them is offered in a spirit of eager joy. They all, without exception, have shown a truly religious and ecumenical attitude of mind. It is for this reason that the Secretariate deplores all utterances that have been made in a spirit at odds with that in which loyal contacts have been established with the observer-delegates. The Secretariate cannot but dissociate itself from those utterances."

This statement alluded to a manifesto of the Ukrainian bishops in exile, excerpts from which had been published on November 21 by the Roman daily *Giornale d'Italia*. It is true, the Ukrainian bishops had not signed the manifesto, and there is a rumor that a secretary released it for publication without their authorization. However, the bishops did not formally repudiate the content of the manifesto either. In it they deplored the absence of their metropolitan, Archbishop Slipyi of Lwów (who has been—these last fifteen years—in a Siberian labor camp). They explained that members of the Orthodox Patriarchate of

Moscow had had a part in the suppression of this Uniat Catholic Church and in the incorporation into the Orthodox Church of the Uniat Christians who had, under duress, abjured their faith. It is for this reason that the Ukrainian bishops present at the Council went on to state in their manifesto: "The presence of two observer-delegates of the Patriarchate of Moscow has confused the faithful, has aroused amazement on the part of not a few Fathers of the Council, and has spread among the clergy and the laity entrusted to our care a feeling of unrest, of dissatisfaction, and of discouragement . . . The Patriarchate of Moscow is a docile and useful instrument of the Soviet government . . . For this reason the dispatch of observers cannot be regarded as a measure of religious and ecclesiastic character but only as a move, alien to all religion, carried out by the Soviet regime with the objective of instigating confusion."

If one compares this Ukrainian manifesto as it appeared in the *Giornale d'Italia* (and from where it was extensively quoted in the world press) with the wording of the statement read by Monsignore Willebrands, there can be little doubt as to whom he had in mind: The Ukrainian bishops and the press which had lent them a helping hand. Immediately after the publication of the manifesto Italian and anticommunist publications elsewhere in the world reported that the observers from Moscow had threatened to leave if the Secretariate did not take a stand against the Ukrainians who had insulted their Patriarch, had attacked the Soviet regime, and had permitted themselves the insinuation that the dispatch of the Moscow observers was a political maneuver of the Soviet government. (German papers had quite frankly interpreted the situation in this latter sense immediately after the dispatch of Russian observers had become known.)

And so it happened. The statement of the Secretariate was an unmitigated disavowal of the Ukrainian bishops, issued for the sake of undisturbed relations with the Russian observers and the Patriarchate of Moscow. The Catholic Church invited them, welcomed them joyfully, and acknowledges their religious and ecumenical attitude of mind.

I do not know who in Rome is so greatly interested in maintaining close relations with the Patriarchate in Moscow and in giving the communist clique in power in the Kremlin no cause to feel hurt. The rightist press in Italy puts the blame on Cardinal Bea. Other circles have the impression that Monsignore Willebrands, acting under the influence of the World Council of Churches or its general secretary but, in any event, at his own initiative, took up the relationship with Moscow and came up with established facts before the Cardinal knew what was happening. According to this interpretation, the Cardinal then found it impossible to change the course that had thus been taken. However all this may have come to passs, I find it difficult to understand—in terms of the politics of the Church—this attitude toward the Uniat Ukrainians. Could it mean that what is wanted is peace with the Patriarchate of Moscow and its political henchmen at the expénse of the suffering Catholic brothers in Russia? That would be a numbers game in Church politics (of the kind we Protestants know only too well from the tactical maneuvers of the World Council of Churches and German Protestant churchmen). It would run something like this: "The fifty-five million Orthodox whom we wish to win over are more important to us for the moment than the more or less lost five million Catholic Ukrainians of the Byzantine-Ukrainian rite in the catacombs of Russia with their one surviving bishop Slipyi." How can one accept such calculations? That, I should think, is hardly the apostolic way of dealing with suffering brothers and their suppressors (especially if these suppressors claim to be themselves the Church of Jesus Christ). Until now we thought that it was the questionable prerogative of Geneva to pursue ecumenical work and efforts of Christian unification at the expense of Christian charity and Christian truth.[22]

At this time Archbishop Slipyi had not as yet been set free. This happened only a short time later. On orders from the Pope the Ukrainian bishops had withheld their signatures. One of the otherwise submissive conservatives must have leaked the text to the Italian press (probably a member of the former Holy Office).

To be sure, the "numbers game" which Lackmann found so objectionable was not at all as unheard-of as he thought. But this will concern us in a later context. For the moment let us take up the interview which Archpriest Borovoi—one of the two Russian observers—gave the journalist and reporter Eva Maria Jung. It was published in the form of a verbatim transcript of the conversation, with the Archpriest speaking first:

"On the occasion of a visit of Monsignore Willebrands to the meeting of the Central Committee of the World Council of Churches in Paris in August 1962, Archbishop Nikodim and I suggested to Monsignore Willebrands that if Rome wished us to be present a personal invitation would have to be extended to us. With all due respect to the Patriarch of Constantinople, we are an independent Church. Monsignore Willebrands asked whether his visit in Moscow would be welcome and we replied that, in case he wished to come, he would be cordially received. After that we waited. The month of August went by and almost all of September, and there still was no word from him. Suddenly we were informed by telegram that Monsignore Willebrands would arrive in Moscow the following day. We greeted him warmly. I was called in from Leningrad for the occasion . . . Monsignore Willebrands stayed with us for six days. In fact, he spoke to a group of members of the Holy Synod. But the invitation was not forthcoming. Monsignore Willebrands explained that he would first have to know whether we were willing to accept his invitation. We replied that we could not reach a decision without having the invitation in our hands. Willebrands left empty-handed and promised to let us know as soon as he reached Rome."

"Allow me to ask in passing: Did either the Vatican or you set up conditions? I mean in the matter of dispatching or receiving observers."

"Conditions? I do not understand what you have in mind. How can one Church stipulate conditions in its dealings with another?"

"Then another question: Did Constantinople know about these negotiations?"

"It knew about them since August. On October 6 we received by wire an inquiry from Athenagoras as to what we were planning to do. But the only reply we could make was, 'We have nothing new to report.' We still had had no word from Rome. The official invitation arrived only the day before the opening of the Council. The Holy Synod was immediately convened and decided to send two observers, and this decision was published that very same evening. We were convincd that we would find in Rome observers representing the Greek Patriarchate. You can imagine how disappointed we are to find ourselves alone."

"Do you think they may still come?"

"We do not know but we hope so."

"And why is it that the other Orthodox Churches that depend on Moscow are not here? For instance the Rumanian Church and the Bulgarian Church."

"There you have it, they do not depend on Moscow. Otherwise they would have come. They are as independent as we are. It seems that the Roman Church still refuses to understand this point."

"But did not Athenagoras explain that his decision to send no observers was reached in consultation with all the Orthodox Churches? How does that jibe?"

"No consultations with us, at least. Athenagoras did inform us of his decision by wire on October 10. But this news reached us only after we had published our decision to send two observers, and it was no longer possible for us to go back on our word. We were struck speechless when we heard of the measure taken by Athenagoras. After all, just a short time ago he had publicly expressed his sympathies for the Council. The first among us to see the wire could not trust his eyes and handed it on for translation to another whose Greek is better. You see, if there were a committee of Orthodox Churches consisting of representatives of all the independent units in the world of Orthodoxy, this misunderstanding could not have happened. All information and all statements of opinion would immediately make the rounds and be discussed. We keep insisting that such a committee should be established, but Athenagoras has not so far seen fit to take any steps in this direction." 23

But let us return to the numbers game which Lackmann found so distasteful. We must try to visualize what would happen if the Orthodox Churches were again united with the Catholic Church. Considerations of this kind underlie all the exchanges and mutual dealings of the Vatican and the Kremlin. They are of decisive significance.

The original concept of this reunion—held up to the time of Pius XII—was extremely simple: The schismatics will see that they were wrong, will ruefully come to heel and "submit." The Holy Office will then have the job of making sure that they do not again stray from the path of the right faith, and the Congregation of Rites will supervise their liturgy. This imperialist attitude, which was seriously considered to be Christian, was abandoned by John XXIII. With some exceptions, the understanding has won out that the "schismatics" and "heretics" possess truths which the Roman Church has suppressed on more than one occasion. There is thus the expectation of a gain. In the case of the Orthodox, this might well be the much-vaunted "collegiality of the bishops."

In concrete terms this signifies that an Orthodox Church can be integrated with the Roman Catholic Church only if it is allowed a far-reaching autonomy (in matters of the liturgy, Church law, and the like). That the Patriarch of Moscow or the Patriarch of Constantinople might accept from a Cardinal of the Curia, or perhaps even from a prelate, prescriptions concerning the liturgy is an idea no longer held by anyone, not even among members of the former Holy Office. Still, it is conceivable that certain ultimate decisions involving authority over the Patriarchs might be made a prerogative of the Pope. He would thus be competent in an area extending somewhat beyond the implications of a purely honorary primateship. But even this kind of subordination of an Orthodox Church would have incisive consequences. The returned Orthodox Church would have to be granted authority over whatever Uniat group there might be in the area of its original range of powers. An illustration of this is that the *collegium russicum* in Rome would have to be made subservient to the Russian Orthodox Church. As a result this Church would gain an influential foothold in Rome, and that might well prove of great interest to the Soviet government.

However, in intra-ecclesiastic terms, too, the Orthodox would benefit greatly, for their liturgy and, in many respects, their theology as well are fairly petrified. Reform proposals of all sorts lead time and again to a formal approximation of the Catholic Church. This lays the reformers open to the accusation that they are traitors working on behalf of Catholicism—"traitor" is a favorite term with the conservatives of all camps—and so it comes to pass that Orthodoxy remains bogged down in medieval forms. A reunion with the Catholic Church could well restore it to greater elasticity and make it more amendable to reforms. One implication would be a sort of retroactive justification of the forced reunion prior to 1945, and in this roundabout way the Uniat groups in the Soviet Union would be helped.

There was however considerable tension between the Uniat Ukrainians and the Poles, so that an alliance of these two groups —especially during the opening phases of the Council—was fortunately impossible. The conservative Poles were visibly annoyed by the presence of the Russians at the Council, but for the moment they did not translate their feelings into actions. The Ukrainians, on the other hand, provoked the Russians. For this purpose they made use of their St. Josaphat Kuncewicz.

As previously stated, the Orthodox Russians see no particular reason to revere this saint. Then, too, all the liberal-minded members of the Catholic hierarchy had dissociated themselves during the Second Vatican Council from the use of brute force which had been St. Josaphat's preferred method of procedure. It was not, therefore, especially tactful toward the Russians to stress particularly the veneration of this particular saint during the period of the Council. And the Ukrainians found other ways as well to challenge the Russians. They acted in the spirit of those reactionaries who persisted in equating reunion with submission. They invited the bishops present at the Council to take part in a celebration in honor of the relics of St. Josaphat, the "great ecumenical saint."

This phrase, "the great ecumenical saint," was clearly intended to be a provocation. For if what St. Josaphat did was ecumenical, it would follow that the Russians even today, to act in a spirit of ecumenicity, would have to submit without resistance or qualification. Most of the bishops invited did not see through what was going on because they did not know at all what St. Josaphat stands for. For this reason they could not have the slightest idea of what a slap in the face to the Russians was implied in this celebration. The Russian observers at the Council were fully aware of who was pulling what strings, but Moscow concluded that the Church of Rome had gone back to its old imperialist way of doing things and that it was intent upon humiliating the Russians. The Russian observers were thus ordered to leave the Council in protest. They tried to explain to their superiors in Moscow that the wire-pullers in Rome were only a small clique, and they were finally permitted to stay on.

The Ukrainian bishops organized the celebration of the final laying to rest of St. Josaphat's relics for November 25, 1963. Then —like a bolt of lightning from a clear sky—arrived the news of the assassination of President Kennedy, the first Catholic President of the USA, whose love of peace was generally recognized. This was an incomparably more important event than the entombment of the bones of St. Josaphat. Most of the bishops therefore went to the requiem celebrated by Cardinal Spellman, and only a small number of undeterred and undeterrable paid St. Josaphat a belatedly last honor.

The ceremony for St. Josaphat was held in St. Peter's, the

requiem for John F. Kennedy—murdered in Dallas, most probably by right-wing extremist conspirators—in the second-rate Lateran basilica. Kennedy—though, strictly speaking, excommunicated by the terms of the notorious syllabus, because he had upheld the principle of the separation of Church and state—represented a truly ecumenical attitude, a spirit of genuine interhuman encounter. Pope Paul VI apparently was not able to see which of the two celebrations was the more important, or —perhaps—he decided to be a solace to the deserted Council fathers in their solitude, for he honored the solemnities for St. Josaphat through his presence. It would seem, however, that he was not quite aware of the awkward way in which the occasion fitted in with the ecumenical spirit. In any event, the vast majority of the bishops was in the Lateran basilica in order to pray there for the dead layman who, after all, had carried a burden of responsibilities heavier than that of hundreds of bishops.

The importance of the coincidence of the two events should not be underrated. If the Russians had left Rome because of the provocation, the other Orthodox groups attending the Second Session as newcomers would likewise have been obliged to leave the Council as a token of solidarity. That might very well have endangered the meeting of Paul VI and Athenagoras in Jerusalem.

Whoever in his personal life has had the experience that in a decisive crisis, at the climactic point of a concatenation of complexities, a solution presented itself of a sudden through a course-shifting occurrence, has derived from that experience the awareness of the logical continuity in his destiny. He cannot, to be sure, survey the complete pattern and cannot understand it in its entirety, but he does find himself in possession of a definitive proof of the existence of a higher power. A man who has found in such an experience the belief in God has simultaneously found the belief in Providence, in a superior intelligence that will reach its objectives in the end despite all human foibles and inadequacies, despite the sabotage of human interference. In world history, too, there are times when we can sense the reality of a meaningful plan. The assassination of the first Catholic President of the United States who wanted peace with the Russians was instigated, no doubt, by a group of reactionaries. In Rome it had the remarkable effect that another reactionary plan wound up in failure. Of course, one may call all this "pure coincidence." Yet, there are those amongst us who find "pure coincidence" a wholly unsatisfactory label. They see a divine plan in the fact that an American President died for peace between Rome and Moscow.

The crisis passed. By releasing Archbishop Slipyi a few weeks later Khrushchev provided one more proof of his interest in reconciliation. By now, however, the Russians had fulfilled their assignment. During the Second Session of the Council various observers representing other Orthodox Churches had arrived in Rome, and Pope Paul VI met Athenagoras of Constantinople in Jerusalem. Finally, at the conclusion of the Council, the mutual excommunication of Rome and Byzantium was solemnly revoked. This was, to be sure, little more than a token of friendliness, for the original excommunications were, to say the least, of doubtful validity. What Orthodox and what Catholic would wish to maintain that all Catholics or all the Orthodox had been in error when they thought they were partaking of the Eucharist?

Although the Russians had initially been considerably less than enthusiastic about participating in the Council, their attitude soon changed. They found that the vast majority of the bishops had not the slightest interest in terrorizing them. They lost much of their distrust. In the process their attitude toward the Uniat groups likewise changed. After all, the Uniats at least spoke their language and to a large extent shared their concepts in historical matters. As a result even the *collegium russicum* ceased to be in their eyes an establishment of anti-Orthodox orientation. To be sure, the point was never explicitly discussed but there is strong evidence to suggest that the question of a reunion with the Church of Rome was seriously considered. For the Patriarch of Moscow, such a reunion would have meant two things: There would have been a certain curtailment of his powers because he would have had to recognize the authority of the Pope in at least some respects, but there would also have

been a considerable increase in his powers since the Uniat groups
would have been placed under Orthodox rule.

One would think that as vast an ecclesiastic organization as
the Russian Orthodox Church would, in case of its reunion with
Roman Catholicism, have to have a "representative" church
building in the immediate vicinity of the Vatican. In matters of
representation, the Orthodox distinguished themselves as little
as the Roman Catholics by imitating the poverty of Jesus Christ.
A Byzantine church would naturally be the most suitable, not a
modern church. Rome has many houses of worship to choose
from. When the metropolitan Nikodim was in Rome he stated
that the one church he like best was Santa Maria Maggiore. This
is one of the largest churches of Rome, a basilica with magnificent Byzantine frescoes—and it is hardly more than 200 yards
away from the *collegium russicum*. Indeed, such details would
have to be worked out in case of a reunion of the Orthodox
Churches with the Church of Rome. In any event, the *collegium
russicum* would have to be integrated with the Orthodox organization.

The reunion of the Russian Church and the Church of Rome
. . .—That is a worthy visionary objective for the diplomats of
the Vatican. It is an objective that will always be assigned a place
of honor in the history of the Church—and also in the College of
Cardinals. Monsignore Casaroli, one of the most intelligent diplomats of the State Secretariate, has been learning Russian for
years. Will the Russians disrupt the Orthodox phalanx for a
second time? This is a most delicate question, for while the answer depends on the Russian Orthodox, it also involves a great
many other factors. If one dares to prognosticate on a long-term
basis, one must take into consideration the complex of multi-
farious interests in which the problem is imbedded.

* * *

Let us first consider Russian Orthodoxy, and in doing so let
us set aside for the moment the part it must play within the
framework of Soviet foreign policies. In Rome no one believes

nowadays that an integration of the Orthodox with the Roman Catholics could be achieved without granting them in a great many respects a degree of autonomy exceeding by far that enjoyed by the Uniat Eastern Churches. Indeed, the various Orthodox patriarchs would have to be granted positions of influence in Rome exceeding that of the average cardinal or even that of a cardinal of the Curia. The matter is somewhat simplified by the fact that there is no Uniat Russian patriarch. One may assume, however, that every now living Orthodox patriarch would have sufficient tact not to insist on the total abdication of a Uniat patriarch if there were such a one.

Some thought has been given to the possibility of reactivating the "Patriarch of the West," that is to say, of separating his functions from those of the Pope. All this goes to show that there is a great deal of good will. It appears, furthermore, that the great fear the Russian Orthodox used to have of the possibility of being terrorized by Rome is no longer extant. If the Orthodox Church retains its autonomous structure and its hierarchical organization, it would have the possibility of revoking the union if ever Rome were to relapse into its former vice of wanting to rule by force. The risk would not be particularly great, particularly not if it were possible in such a situation to rely on state support, that is to say, on support by the Soviet authorities.

What gains would accrue to the Russian Orthodoxy from a union with Rome: First of all, it would be in a position to exert its influence at the Vatican. At the Second Vatican Council, it was the presence of Russian observers that prevented the condemnation of communism. In this sense the Orthodox could extend their influence, and that would assure them a role of world-wide significance. And this, specifically, is of course a point that is bound to interest the Soviet government. In turn, then, by increasing its influence in extra-Russian affairs, the Russian Church would consolidate its position within Russia and assure its continued existence. It goes without saying that in the process the Russian Church would become more resilient and more inclined to evince an interest in matters of reform.

What now is the position of the Soviet government in this matter? It is in the interest of the communist parties of the West to induce the governments of the eastern people's republics to adopt liberal policies with respect to the Church. There is also the point that the eastern states have developed sizable numbers of intellectuals who demand freedom of thought. These intellectuals are the rulers of the future. For this reason it is not only unthinkable, it is impossible that they should forever be denied the freedom they want. The class in power still has the possibility of keeping the ruled unfree. But once that class recognizes that freedom is in its own interest, the progressive advance toward ever greater freedom becomes a process which nothing can arrest. At the present time freedom of religion is something which the government of the eastern people's democracies can wisely grant or unwisely deny. In a few years that decision will no longer be theirs. Freedom of religion will be demanded and achieved along with the freedom of thought, the freedom of art, and the freedom of science. Numerous communist functionaries are quite aware of these facts. Their way of ruling has come to be free from elements of sadism, and they derive satisfaction from operating on the basis of a broad endorsement by the people.

Finally, an arrangement with the Catholic Church would indirectly open up various tempting possibilities of breaking the "capitalist ring of steel of containment." By way of illustration we need but suggest that a truly strong communist party in Italy might succeed in having that country sever its relations with the NATO Alliance, and there can be little doubt but that anything resembling a concordat of Moscow and Rome would immeasurably strengthen the Italian communists. In any event, what better way is there of gaining influence in Rome than by means of the Orthodox Church? If this provides a sound reason for the Soviet government to meet the Orthodox Church halfway, it also opens up the possibility for the Orthodox Church to represent in Rome the interests of the Soviets with a clearer conscience. Obviously, the Soviets would have no objection whatever to an Orthodox-Catholic union, if the Catholic Church were willing to endorse socialism—if only in the sense of agreeing to the principle of public ownership of the means of production—and thus to reach a decision against capitalism. To be sure, Rome cannot go that far. The Church depends too much on American and also West German money. Catholicism in the United States of America is expanding, and the Church cannot write off its American interests for the sake of mere potentialities in the east. Still, the Vatican is in a position to pay handsomely in various ways (which the Soviets are bound to find profitable) for a liberal Soviet attitude toward the Churches and for a Soviet endorsement of plans for the reunion of Orthodoxy and Catholicism.

One such way would be Rome's backing of the status quo against the revisionist demands still heard in the Federal Republic of Germany (and also in conservative circles in Poland). A guarantee of the status quo would have various implications. First and foremost, the guarantee of the western borders of Soviet Union (and of the German Democratic Republic) would be a concession to the legitimate insistence on safety and security of the Soviet Union. John XXIII did some preparatory work in this sense.

Political efforts in the interest of peace could also bear fruit in that they might result in permanent disarmament. This would lead to a reduction in the extraordinarily high military expenses which represent a real burden to the budgets of the eastern states. As a result, much-needed investments could be diverted to the general economy, and the countries involved would become better able to compete with capitalist producers.

A neutral attitude of the Vatican in the capitalist-socialist tug of war might have—as we have repeatedly pointed out—far-reaching consequences. In fact, the practical effect might be tantamount to an endorsement of the former adversary (as illustrated by the example of the local elections in North Rhine-Westphalia in 1966). In many countries—including Austria, the Federal Republic of Germany, and others—the liberal-conservative parties derive their strength from the Catholics and other Christian groups. It is not at all rare that Christian workers vote a conservative ticket against their class interests because the party that does represent those interests is atheistic or is reputed to be atheistic or even anti-Christian. This group of voters, by the way, represents the potential mass backing for the left-wing Catholic intellectuals who wage a war on two fronts: Against the affiliation of the Church with the upper classes and against the association of atheism with the parties representing the economically less privileged.

We must look at the situation from the point of view of the Vatican rather than from an Austrian, Swiss, American or—worst of all—a Federal-German point of view. Particularly those countries are of importance in this respect which are currently in the throes of critical processes of fermentation, such as the countries of South America or of Africa. An attitude of neutralism on the part of the Catholic Church in the conflict of the socialistic and capitalistic systems would, in large areas of South America, have precisely the same practical effect which the Church's siding with socialism would have. Something similar —as intimated—applies to Italy, in part also to France, and—in the last analysis—even to Spain. It is hence by no means paradoxical for the Kremlin to strive seriously to come to some sort of an arrangement with the Catholic Church. A reunion of the Church of Rome with the Russian Church would in this respect be a step forward. There can be no question but that the time has come not only for the people's democracies but also for the Soviet Union to take up the question of the Church and to abandon the rigid attitude of conservative communism.

From the point of view of the Church, an arrangement with communism and the resulting integration of the Russian Church would open up two possibilities of high-powered significance. On the one hand, the Church would have the very appealing possibility of gaining a foothold in the new communist world which, to be sure, is currently on the defensive but which, nonetheless, has a promising future. On the other hand, the integration of the Russian Church would not only be the fulfillment of an ancient dream of Vatican endeavor but, indeed, much more. Once this first ecumenical objective has been achieved, the remaining Orthodox Churches would find it hardly possible to maintain for themselves an existence separate from the Roman Church. And the Russians would doubtless do a great deal in the interest of a Catholic universalism if the treaty of reunion were sufficiently bolstered with clauses providing security against all possible forms of centralistic arrogation. The implication is that the Catholic world would undergo a certain degree of decentralization.

However, the problem—as seen from the point of view of the Vatican—is dichotomous and represents, in a sense, a classical dilemma. The mere readiness of the Vatican to enter into negotiations with communist governments outside of Italy weakens the resistance of that country against communism, and Italy is —for understandable reasons—a country which plays a major role in the thinking of the Vatican. Yet, if the Italian communists succeed in taking over even a fraction of the powers of the government before an international understanding on basic issues has been achieved, the result would be a substantial weakening of the Vatican's bargaining position. The Vatican knows that it is bad business to pay before one knows what it is one has bought. But this danger—at least at present—does not seem to be too terribly real. The Italian communists will not find that the Vatican extends them a helping hand unless and until they succeed in inducing their comrades in the east to pursue more liberal policies in Church matters. If and when—but only if and when—the Italian Communist Party undertakes steps in this direction, will its policies bear international fruit.

The Vatican and Poland

The historical development in the east of Europe represents— as does any historical continuity—a complex of interactions and dependencies. For this reason it was unavoidable for our discussion of the Vatican-Russian relations to include repeated references to the Vatican-Polish and, especially, the Polish-Russian relations. As one attempts to focus one's attention on the factor Poland in this complex, one finds that the German-Polish relations are likewise of crucial significance. In the traditional Polish-Russian conflict, the Poles were initially the aggressors and the Russians the victims. In the traditional German-Polish conflict it was primarily the Germans who had the role of the aggressors. Quite clearly there was an economic and technological gradient inviting expansion eastward. After Russia had come of age, Poland found itself wedged in between two great powers which divided it at their mutual will. However, these partitions of Poland must not be overrated in their significance.

Within the Catholic realm, Poland's past represents a rather unusual tradition. In terms of its constitution the country was to a large extent a liberal monarchy. The lower nobility elected the king. Since there were a great many lower nobles, the number of individuals with voting rights was often relatively large. The kings of Poland did not inherit their claims to the throne. It was, therefore, of great interest to them to have their sons elected kings, and to that end they made increasingly important concessions to the electors. In this way the elective kingdom of Poland was resting on a basis entailing a certain democratic element.

The early position of the Primate of Poland is crucially important for an understanding of the Polish situation at the present time. The Primate was interrex, that is, he was invested with royal powers during the interregnum. Just as in the Holy Roman Empire the Prince Electors were subject to external influences at the time of the election of a new emperor in ways often hard to differentiate from sheer bribery, the Polish situation, too, involved a host of "irregularities" complicating the election procedure and causing—in many instances—considerable delays with all the untoward implications one can imagine. Quite frequently protracted periods of time went by after the death of a king before his successor was finally elected. And these intervals often proved decisive in terms of the subsequent fate of the country.

Until the new king was elected, the Primate of Poland—being interrex—represented the supreme political authority. As one compares the political position of such a primate with that of the primate in an hereditary monarchy, one sees clearly that the latter was bound to have an incomparably smaller political importance, even though he, too, was vested with the powers of an interrex. In an hereditary monarchy, the death of the ruler is followed immediately by the accession of his heir. "The king is dead, long live the king."

In Hungary, which was a feudal state in the full sense of the term, the primate was nonetheless in a position to exert great influence. His cathedral of Esztergom, a small provincial town, was the ostentatious, yet gigantic, symbol of his power. By comparison, the position of the Archbishop of Vienna is of minimal political significance. Ambitions in this direction on the part of the Viennese archbishop—if he had them—would have been kept within narrow bounds by the Hapsburgs who were not inclined to share their political powers with anyone, especially not in the city which was the capital of their empire.

The powers of the primate and interrex of Poland were further increased by the fact that the Roman-Catholic bishops were ex officio voting members of the Sejm, the Polish diet. If one considers how within the Church the tenacious preservation of traditions is often carried to the point of full-fledged absurdity, —in Salzburg, for instance, the title *Primas Germaniae* is still regarded as a potentially useful tool of politics—one cannot see anything astonishing in the political attitudes of a Cardinal Wyszynski.

The distinctive features of Polish Catholicism are related to the fact that the Poles have a genuinely revolutionary tradition. This is remarkable insofar as Catholics, on the whole, are raised in a spirit of obedience, not to say submissiveness. The Poles have become experts in conspiracy against occupying powers and are not inclined to consider every kind of authority God-willed and hence sacrosanct. To be sure, the revolutionary impulse is quite often unrealistic in terms of the evaluation of its own possibilities and of the possibilities of others and will, hence, lead not infrequently to acts of meaningless self-sacrifice. But the ability to oppose authorities with an unmistakable "No" raises Polish Catholicism typically high above the Catholicism of, for instance, Germany or Austria. This is not meant to imply that Polish Catholicism is devoid of foibles and weaknesses. Up to the time of the Second World War, Poland was essentially a feudal state. Styles and standards of life and of thinking were determined by the landed aristocracy. It is not at all far-fetched to suggest that the blood baths wreaked by the Tatars on the cities inhibited the full development of the emergent bourgeoisie. The Polish nobles were brave to the point of being foolhardy, but in matters of technology, science, and economics, they could hardly keep pace with the bourgeoisies of the West.

Polish Catholicism is likewise—in its intellectualization—more than a little retarded compared to that of other countries. To be sure, there are eminent Catholic intellectuals, but the broad Catholic masses are involved in a type of Mariolatry which is at times reminiscent of conditions in South America. The situation is beautifully characterized by the following story which—unfortunately—is told to characterize the Russian mentality, but it could be and, in fact, ought to be Polish. At one time the Russian town of Zagorsk was attacked by Polish knights. The attack failed, and the defenders declared that this was proof positive that the Madonna of Zagorsk was stronger than that of Czestochowa.—The most urgent need for Polish Catholicism would be its intellectualization and not a further strengthening of its Mariolatry.

As we consider the relations between the Poles and the Vatican throughout the course of history, we cannot but be impressed by the fact the Poles were dealt with unfairly on more than one occasion. To be sure, as far as their conflict with the Russians is concerned, they were the attackers, but the subsequent suppression of the legitimate national interests of the Poles by the Russians went certainly too far. In any event, since Poland lost its position as a great power through the several partitions of the country, its interests were neglected by the Vatican, too.

In modern times Pius XII hastened in this spirit to recognize Hitler's conquests in Poland, for he kept hoping that Hitler's troops would open the way for Catholicism's advance into Russia. Parts of the so-called Warthegau (along the Warta river) were annexed to German dioceses and hence placed under German bishops. This was a breach of the Polish concordat with the Vatican which stipulated that Polish territory should never be placed under the administration of foreign bishops.

Today the Vatican refuses to recognize the formerly German areas east of the Oder-Neisse line as de-jure Polish territory because—so the argument runs—it is a tradition of the Vatican to wait for peace treaties and to establish definitive diocesan boundaries only on the basis of their terms. This is clearly a case of judging by dual standards. The National Socialists were clearly, in the eyes of Pius XII, something better than the Bolsheviks. The governments of Western Germany and of Austria appear to be still of that opinion. As a matter of fact, the Polish interests continue to this day to be regarded as less important than the German interests. There is evidence of an impending change in this situation, but whatever happens in this area, the deeds of the past will not thereby be undone.

The relations of the Poles with the Germans determine not only Polish politics but also that of the Soviets and of the Czechs. The existence of two German states, the Federal Republic of Germany and the German Democratic Republic, represents a special problem. It arose originally from the objective of the Allies to keep the potential aggressor Germany from regaining its strength. The partition of Germany in two states with different ideological bases reduces the possibility of a renewed excessive concentration of power in the center of Europe and hence of a resumption of the German expansion toward the east and the southeast. It also represents for the Western nations a certain guarantee that the economic expansion of Germany will stay within manageable limits. In practice, of course, it is not particularly easy to implement such plans of management and control. We need but think of the expansion of German capital in Austria and the Netherlands.

From the point of view of the Soviet Union it was of great importance to subject the states in the buffer zone beyond its western boundaries to its own influence to such a degree that they could never again serve—as did Hungary and Rumania under Hitler—as the bases for an attack on the Soviet Union. This implied that the German Democratic Republic had to be integrated with the eastern bloc by ties that could not possibly be severed.

Yet the Federal Republic kept claiming that it alone could speak for the Germans. This self-appraisal led to the formulation of the Hallstein Doctrine with its gangster-like arguments—not even the USA insists that its allies must not recognize Peking— and to the demand that the borders of 1938 be restored. Franz Josef Strauss, in fact, did not hesitate to intimate that another *Anschluss* of Austria might not be a bad thing at all. Individual representatives of the West German government insisted—with characteristic modesty—that ultimately the Sudeten territory would have to be "returned" to Germany (although before the First World War it belonged to Austria). At least with respect to this last point, the Kiesinger government has finally taken a clear stand.

Such a catalog of demands cannot but force every Polish and every Czech government to side with the Soviet Union. In fact, the USSR did not have to force the governments of those two countries to follow a certain line in their foreign politics. It is much rather the overall constellation which dictates that line. To the Poles and the Czechs the idea that the German Democratic Republic might be turned over to the Federal Republic of Germany is entirely unacceptable. From a sense of moral solidarity it is impossible for them to drop the ruling clique of the German Democratic Republic with its faithful adherence to the east, and they do not believe that an all-German state—combining the third largest industrial potential of the world (the Federal Republic of Germany) with the eleventh largest (the German Democratic Republic)—would keep the peace, even if it were to sign a peace treaty stipulating its recognition of the present borders. As long as the Federal Republic of Germany does not provide proof positive of its lasting will to peace (renunciation of atomic arms, unconditional disarmament, and the like), the possibility of permitting a reunification of Germany is naturally out of the question from the point of view of the Eastern bloc. But the West, too, would find it extremely embarrassing if the Soviets were suddenly ready to agree to a German reunification. It is quite sound to insist that the West would not support the German demands if it were not convinced that a rejection of those demands by the Soviets can be relied upon.

All these reflections depend on whether one considers communism and the communist states to be transitional phenomena that can somehow be destroyed or realities that are here to stay. The hope cherished by Pius XII that National Socialism could be used in breaking open the east for a Catholic invasion was an extremely dangerous illusion. Had Hitler been victorious he would have given short shrift to the Catholic Church, this "off-

spring of Judaism." Pius XII, in his political "far-sightedness,"
was at best a dilettante. To be sure, Father Leiber, S.J., secretary
to Pius XII, explained that the Pope considered communism the
more dangerous adversary because in many respects it had to
be taken more seriously, but this is certainly less than the whole
truth. Pius XII was a born ruler, a *prince* of the Church in the
full sense of the term, and this established, in a way, congenial
bonds between him and National Socialism, while "proletarian"
communism was basically alien to him. He was of the opinion
that orders and decrees issued by the (spiritual) leaders could
solve all problems of mankind. He despised democracy and, indeed, believed in the value of "noble" blood.

In the *Roman Notebook* of Tadeusz Breza I find the following
passage:

Prince Luigi P. told me yesterday at M's that his cousin, at a gala
reception in Paris, had observed two gentlemen sitting next to him
deeply absorbed in their conversation. One of them was Aga Khan, the
other Cardinal Eugenio Pacelli, Secretary of State of the Roman Church
who later on became Pope. Aga Khan was in the habit of spending
several months of each year in Paris, and Pacelli had come back from
England where he had been Papal Legate to a eucharistic congress.
Prince P.'s cousin could not resist the temptation of listening in on the
conversation between the man who was the right hand of Christ's
representative on earth and the descendant and representative of Mo-
hammed.

It appears that the representative and future absolute head of four
hundred million Catholics and the head of one hundred million
Ismaelites were talking about horses and, specifically, about thoroughbreds. Aga Khan insisted that the superiority of thoroughbreds was, to a
certain extent, a myth and that he for one had made millions on the
race track with horses that did not have uncontaminated pedigrees but
instead talent, fire, and training. Pacelli replied that he considered such
gains accidental strokes of good fortune. He regarded the advantages of
pure blood, of a good pedigree, and of "noble" breeding as matters of
law confirmed by innumerable experiences in history. Particularly where
the human race is involved. [24]

If this report is not true, it is at any rate an excellent invention which beautifully fits the "aristocratic" demeanor of this
Pope.

Since Pius XII meant to use Hitler to hit the Bolsheviks, he had to sacrifice the Polish interests. For this reason he is not at all popular in Poland. Indeed, in wide circles in Poland one cannot mention his name without arousing violent opposition.

Pius was unhappy about the total German defeat. He was opposed to the demand of an unconditional surrender because he wanted to preserve the German potential for the struggle against the Bolsheviks. As a matter of fact, Roosevelt's insistence on Germany's unconditional surrender was absolutely right. Ignaz Seipel once remarked unofficially: "The Allies in 1918 should have marched through the Brandenburg Gate to make sure that the Germans understood that they had really lost the war." [25] Despite the defeat of 1945 and the unconditional surrender, it is only now that wide circles in the Federal Republic of Germany "really understand" that Germany lost the war, if "really understand" can be defined as implying "to act accordingly."

The mass murders of the Nazis did have a sobering effect on Pius's Germanophilia, but his misevaluation of communism remained intact. He clearly expected an armed clash between east and west. While he had not objected to Catholic cooperation with the National Socialists—at the decisive moment in history, in 1933, he paralyzed the Catholic Center in Germany in favor of Hitler—he opposed categorically every kind of understanding between Catholics and communists. Hitler's *Mein Kampf,* which states among other things that mixing of races is the "original sin," [26] was never placed on the Index. Catholics were never officially forbidden to join the National Socialist Party, but Catholic members of the Communist Party were excommunicated. Of the Germans Pius did not demand that they become martyrs in the resistance movement against Hitler, but he did expect martyrdom from the Catholics in communist countries.

A typical illustration is the case of Archbishop Beran in Prague. Originally Beran had favored an arrangement with the communists who had come to power in Czechoslovakia in 1948. After Gottwald had been elected president, Beran recited the Te Deum at the Cathedral of St. Vitus, and Gottwald was the first president of Czechoslovakia to attend such a celebration. But then Beran was urged by the Vatican to assume an attitude of recalcitrance. In those days the ideas prevalent at the Vatican with respect to what the future might bring were quite different from what they are today. After the anticipated east-west clash, the Catholics were to arise—after their ordeal of communist oppression—like a phoenix from its ashes.

Everywhere in the east there were bishops, priests, and Christian laymen who were better prepared to understand the situation than Pius XII. They considered his policies and his evaluation of communism to be wrong. They believed neither in the ephemerality of communism nor in the inevitability of an east-west war. Many of them had met communists in German concentration camps and felt linked to them in solidarity as brothers in arms against National Socialism. They strove to come to an understanding with the regime, they believed in a humane core in communism, and they persisted in the hope—rightly so—that the future was bound to lead to a "humanization" of communism. But before long such people came to be regarded in Rome as traitors. It was not quite clear whether the decree of excommunication against communism implied that they, as individuals, were excommunicated, too. This attitude is typically and classically represented by the Catholic groups in Poland, such as the Znak and Pax organizations to which we must add, for the time after Gomulka's accession to power, the Christian-Social society of Frankowski. Of all these organizations, only the Znak has the reputation of enjoying the trust and confidence of Cardinal Wyszynski.

While Archbishop Beran, as a result of his concentration-camp experience, had at first favored an understanding with the communists, Cardinal Mindszenty opposed from the start the pro-communist coalition regime under the leadership of the Small Landholders Party. The Catholic hierarchies in the east were stripped of their powers and made to depend economically on the regime. Only the Polish episcopate came to an agreement with the government as early as 1950. To be sure, in Poland, too, Stalinism took its toll. Several bishops, including the Cardinal, were thrown into prison, but the hierarchical order remained essentially intact.

But then Stalin died. Step by step Khrushchev came to the fore. The era of de-Stalinization began. Tito's conflict with

Stalin had represented the first crack in the monolithic unity of the "socialist camp." The process of "decomposition" continued. For years the naive anti-communist myth of the "red disease" prevented many people from realizing that communists, too, are human beings and hence may get involved in mutual dissent. However, the idea that the communists would eternally remain at one, thus constituting the first example in history of a movement without a built-in potential for divergence, began to lose in credibility, for the first evidence began to appear of the impending Soviet-Chinese schism.

The year 1956 brought the Hungarian revolution which overshot its goal, a fact for which Cardinal Mindszenty was not entirely blameless. In Poland, on the other hand, a genuine breakthrough to freedom proved possible, much of which was preserved throughout the ensuing regressive setbacks. This is due above all to the fact that Stalinism in Poland had never evolved to the extremes seen in other communist states. In Poland the leaders of the liberal wing of communism were not simply liquidated but only locked up, though they were often subjected to torture. Gomulka came out of prison to power. His release coincided with that of Cardinal Wyszynski. It is to the credit of the Russians that they did not intervene in Poland although this country was obviously about to rid itself of the status of a satellite. In this the Russian communists proved politically wiser and morally more mature than the czars, just as the Polish communists proved wiser and more mature than the former Polish nationalists. The Russian czars had tried to destroy the national substance of Poland. The Russian communists, on the other hand, tried nothing of the sort. They also refrained from impeding the national development of Poland, just as they did not impede the national development of Hungary, Rumania, and other people's democracies. The Polish communists, in their turn, practiced moderation, and so did the bishops. It was political acumen that induced Cardinal Wyszynski to side with Gomulka during the crucial days of the Polish October.

There is a story that made the rounds at the time in Poland, relating a conversation between Gomulka and Cardinal Wyszynski. Gomulka said: "I have trouble with Moscow. Could you not get me an excommunication?" Wyszynski replied: "I have trouble with Rome. Could you not get me locked up for a few weeks?"

In Poland elections were held that were tantamount to a plebiscite. Gomulka's followers demanded a "vote of confidence." If the Poles rejected Gomulka, they had to reckon with military action on the part of the Russians, for the Soviets could not afford to lose Poland to the West. Such a loss would have meant the collapse of their entire strategic system of defense. The Poles had to remain within the Russian sphere of influence, but under Gomulka they could anticipate greater freedom. So they remained in the eastern bloc and retained the assurance of help in the event of West German territorial claims. Cardinal Wyszynski supported the election of Gomulka. It would have been possible for him to prevent this election and thus to trigger a catastrophe. By contrast to Cardinal Mindszenty, Cardinal Wyszynski was guided by political reason and wisdom.

This signifies that Gomulka was legitimized by the people. The thesis of many political refugees to the effect that today's Polish government is Moscow's caretaker is wrong. Surely, the present rulers of Poland would not be in the driver's seat if it were not for the Russians. But they would likewise be elsewhere if it were not for the Polish people that backed them up at a crucial moment against the Stalinist Russians. Today Poland is the most important ally of the Soviet Union.

During the Hungarian revolt, the major portion of the Soviet "piloting personnel" understood that the USSR had permitted itself very serious errors in its political dealings with the communist states. For this reason the Soviet leadership was ready to grant major concessions to the national communist groups. However, Cardinal Mindszenty proved unequal to the situation in that he thought it possible to get Hungary to break away from the eastern system, and by insisting on this objective he conjured up the catastrophe.

When after the Polish October state and Church in that country made peace, the Vatican politicians found themselves confronted with a totally new situation. There were now "good" communists whom it was no longer possible to characterize as tools in the hands of the devil. The turn of events in Poland, the transition of that country to the status of a state based on law and constitutional rights, and—above all—its transition to a condition of relative freedom for the Church, produced a very unusual kind of communism. Since man, particularly when he is of a conservative bend of mind, hates to change his ideas, he defends himself against changed realities by means of what psychoanalysis terms "defense mechanisms." The changes in Poland resulted in the most varied reactive defense mechanisms, manifest in a number of diametrically contradictory observations:

"In reality" nothing has changed (negation, repression).

Almost nothing has changed (trivialization).

What the Poles are doing is no longer communism. Gomulka is actually no communist but a socialist (conversion).

Despite everything, the old image of communism proved subject to "metabolic" transformation. Slowly but surely the reorientation got underway.

Considering the later demeanor of Cardinal Wyszynski, one wonders what enabled him in 1956 to take so reasonable a position. The explanation would seem to lie in the fact that in those days he saw the German problem in a different light. His emotional reactions to Russians and Germans were doubtless equally negative. However, the Russians had no claims against the Poles, but the Germans did. For this reason it makes sense to assume that the rejection of the German revisionist demands were uppermost in his thinking. In matters of foreign politics the Cardinal depended on the Russians and thus on the Polish communists who represented the bridge to the Russians. In their defensive attitude toward a potential German aggression the Catholics and the communists had a common basis. In Hungary, on the other hand, there was no shared interest between Catholics and communists in matters of foreign policy.

Since under Pius XII the Vatican's foreign policies were geared to the objective of eastern expansion, a conflict with the policies of the Polish episcopate seemed unavoidable. There was also the fact that Pius backed the revisionist demands of the Federal Republic of Germany. The growing numbers of communist votes in Italy made it impossible for the Vatican to heed the eighth commandment and honor truth above all. A communist could never be anything but a communist in precisely the sense first attributed to the term. If the possibility had been acknowledged that there can be good communists and bad communists, the idea might have gotten a foothold in Italy that the Italian communists need not necessarily be condemned on all scores. In fine, the Polish situation endangered the simplistic black-and-white picture of communism that was propagated by the Vatican.

In Breza's *Roman Notebook,* quoted once before, there is the transcript of a conversation that author had with a high-ranking personality whom he did not feel free to identify, but whom he described in an introductory paragraph:

He belongs to the small circle of the Pope's closest or, shall we say, private non-ranking and untitled collaborators. He is never far from where the Pope is, and this has been so for many years. He does not associate much with others, for whatever he says may quickly turn into a rumor. He is, in the minds of all who know him, the quintessence of aloofness and silence. That he came to be affiliated with Eugenio Pacelli was in the cards. It happened a long time ago. If Fate had a hand in it, it is the same fate that placed the other better-known men—Father Robert Leiber and Father Wilhelm Hentrich—in this circle. All three— of late a fourth name has come to be added to the list—are Jesuits, and all come from Southern Germany. The youngest of them all is the man with whom I had yesterday's conversation. He is seventy-six. He first met the Pope before he (Eugenio Pacelli) was even a bishop . . .

I began the conversation with an apology for making such a claim on his time.

"I have made arrangements to be able to carry on this conversation," he replied.

I once again expressed my gratitude for his having found time for me and began the conversation proper by assuring him that I intended to speak to him exclusively as a private individual.

"I need not stress this point particularly," he replied, "a private individual is all I am."

Private or not, our conversation took a political turn. He expressed his interest in, as he put it, "What your people think about the Vatican."

"Who?" I asked, "Those at the top?"

"Those at the very top."

"They are not enthusiastic about it, and they also do not know it very well."

"Do they know what the Vatican thinks of them?"

"No."

"Why then do they not ask their Cardinal?"

"Cardinal Wyszynski?"

"Of course."

"Does Cardinal Wyszynski know what the Vatican thinks about them?"

"He most certainly does. If these people want to know more about the Vatican, he can serve as the authoritative source of all information."

I explained why the matter was not quite that simple. From the Vatican's point of view, communism, I said, was the greatest evil of our time which had to be fought day and night on all fronts. One of the top commanders, Cardinal Wyszynski, did conclude an armistice along his sector of the front. This happened because along that commander's sector conditions came to be such as to make an armistice desirable and even necessary. It was an armistice that had an excellent chance of evolving into a lasting peace. But, I concluded, one could not expect—particularly not today—that the commanders of the forces on the other side of the front would come to the cardinal to learn from him what the intentions of the Vatican might be.

"But they trust him."

"That is true."

"So?"

"In the struggle with those on the other side he continues to be the embodiment of a party."

The man before me said: "The most important question is whether Warsaw realizes that the Holy Father accepts without qualification the guiding principles underlying the actions of your cardinal."

"No, that is not realized, and it would not be believed."

"Yet, he does accept them without any kind of *reservatio mentalis*. He accepts them as wise and believes that the cardinal may follow them forever. He himself, that is the Pope, has always accepted them. It would be very important if the men in Warsaw could be made to clearly understand this."

I expressed my amazement at what he had told me. In Warsaw, I explained, no one among the leaders would give credence to such assurances. After all, the day-to-day practice of the Vatican had taught them better. Furthermore, the day-to-day practice was what found expression in semiofficial political utterances, in fully official declarations, and in the Vatican-directed press. All this, I summed up, signified that the attitude of the Vatican toward Poland was as negative today as it had always been. As in the past, so today, too, our particular and specific religious situation is not heeded.

"That is no easy problem," he answered. "It would not be entirely unrisky to suddenly come out enthusiastically for Gomulka as a new thinker and reformer of Marxism."

"But it would not seem to be asking too much to expect the Vatican not to make a secret of what has happened between the Church and the state in Poland. In fact, however, the Vatican not only makes a secret of it, it depicts these things in a way that is not true and does so through the most authoritative voices. I am thinking, for instance, of the most recent prayer for 'the silent Church' or the address on the occasion of the inauguration of the new transmitter of the Vatican."

"And why, in your opinion, should the Holy Father speak differently?"

Because, I said in essence, the only point that matters is that the delicate relations we are discussing have become normalized. Every normalization of such relations—every example of a local solution of antinomies previously regarded as irresolvable—advances us as well as the Vatican by another step along the road of escape from the catastrophe that could annihilate the earth.

He did not answer, pondering what I had said.

I continued: "I find it astonishing that the political columnist of the *Osservatore Romano,* Allessandrini, keeps repeating the same attacks."

"Let us not talk about unimportant details."

"I mention that paper because you, Father, asked me why Warsaw does not believe that the Pope has accepted the cardinal's line. The answer is that the *Osservatore Romano* is read in Warsaw for precisely the same reason for which the *Times* is being read, with the implication that what appears to be stated between the lines of the *Osservatore Romano* is interpreted in an analogous way."

"One half of every issue of the *Osservatore Romano* goes to the USA, South America, Africa, and the Asians. The North Americans in particular are no Europeans and would not understand complications and nuances. For America everything must be black or white. A communist must be evil in his totality and must persecute the Church. To tell the truth about you would in such areas be tantamount to doing procommunist work."

"But sooner or later the facts will have to be acknowledged," I answered.

"The later the better. I have never believed in the ultimate defeat of communism. I do not believe now in retrospect that communism could have been contained or isolated by iron curtains, mountain ranges, or oceans. It permeates everything and continues to advance. The point is that its progress must be slowed down as much as possible. The ultimate fact is that communism is not antireligious but areligious. It is antireligious only in its storm-and-stress phase, its period of hypervigilance, its time of warlike aggression. Later on, when communism has definitively established itself, it is bound to assume an attitude of indifference toward religion. What matters is that we survive this most difficult interval. Once it has passed, it will be incumbent upon those of us who are still around to 'make yeast' for a totally new epoch."

I asked him whether he had read in the September or October issue of *Etudes,* the monthly of the French Jesuits, the study by J. J. Baumgartner, "La Pologne en quête de son équilibre" [Poland in Quest of Its Equilibrium], in which the author demonstrates that the relations between Church and state in Poland have evolved for the better and in fact for the best. In some respects, I summarized Baumgartner, this relationship had evolved, from the point of view of the Church, in a way that might prove to be extremely fruitful. Through the fact that the Church in Poland is no large landed proprietor and no financial power, the church there is not separated from the working man's world in the way leading elsewhere to the loss of the proletariat which Pius XI called the scandal of the nineteenth century.

No, he had not read that essay. As for the concluding thesis I had quoted, he considered it sound, particularly from an historical point of view. This point of view, by the way, was—he explained—distinctively congenial to the French Jesuits, both in intellectual and material terms, for they came predominantly from the poorest provinces of the country. For the American Jesuits, on the other hand, such a view would be totally impossible. In America, where one third of all Jesuits are located, it would be considered quixotic at best and tantamount to sheer demagoguery at worst. Not because the American Jesuits are the tools of millionaires but because all their work depends exclusively on their enormous revenues. They work dynamically and with a tremendous organizational sense of conquest. Their missions are to be found in Africa, Asia, Oceania, the Philippines, Taiwan, Korea, and Japan, they creep into every hole which the British, the French, and the Dutch have relinquished. They are Catholic missionaries in postcolonial areas which they regard as post-Protestant or postsecular. They work for America to the same extent as the Spanish Jesuits of the age of Philip II or the

Portuguese of the Order of Aviz worked for Spain or Portugal. It would be senseless to try to convince them that the Church or their order ought to be poor. In particular, it would be impossible to convince them—even though it be true that a poor priest is better qualified than a rich one to convert a working man—that a member of a colored race can be won for the Church more easily by a poor missionary than by a rich one.

In reply to all this I remarked that I had the impression that both intellectually and spiritually he had deeper sympathies for the French Jesuits than for the Jesuits of America.

"That does not apply to me alone," he said. "But I fear that the American Jesuits are more in tune with the times. When, in the more or less foreseeable future, there will be Soviet Jesuits, they too—in a different way—will be more in tune with the present than the French Jesuits. The world of today is unfortunately no longer the world of the declining Roman Empire that was longing for a humanist and mystical gospel. The present world is run by empires of expanding dimensions. There are three of these, possibly four, possibly five: that of the Soviets, that of the Americans, the Chinese, the Indians, and the Indonesian, to disregard the lesser Afro-Asian peoples and political structures. The will to power is everywhere, and everywhere is enthusiasm for technology, for modernization, for the material values of civilization. The modern Church—and our society within it—must adjust itself to the style of the age. Otherwise its voice will no longer be heard by anyone but those inhabitants of Europe who have been hearing it anyway for centuries. Mind you, I do not say that your Baumgartner is wrong. He is right. Yet, in the decisions which the Church has to reach in its day-to-day work, the decisions which the Catholic life of the entire world demands of it, time and again the opposite truth proves itself, and it does so with pre-ponderant cogency. It is for this reason that the Roman Curia cannot wholeheartedly share the joy which the *Etudes* experience in the face of the impecuniousness of the Polish Church. I repeat that I am indeed far from keeping my ears plugged to the arguments of Baumgartner. It is quite possible that the distant future will be his. The immediate future, in any event, belongs to the American Jesuits."

I voiced certain doubts and he continued.

"I am a European through and through. My background, my education, my feelings predestine me for this part of the earth. Yet, on the basis of what I see happening elsewhere I must think in ways contrary to my inborn inclinations. Let me mention but one example, one which is—admittedly—exceptional in its effectiveness. It is the example of Japan. Before the war there were just a handful of Roman Catholic congregations there. Today there are three million Catholics in Japan. In the Philippines, in India, in Indonesia, and even in America Catholicism keeps expanding mightily from year to year. These facts are of decisive importance for the political thinking of the Curia. And, I should assume, for the thinking of the Holy Father, too."

Suddenly he returned to the Polish question. "The news from Poland is very heartening. The Jesuits present at our extraordinary assembly had nothing but good things to say about your government and your communists. They said that no one interfered with their work. All were greatly moved by this fact. I myself talked at length with one of them. I know very well what is happening in your country. I even think I know why it is happening in just this way. I know, for instance, that Monsignore Baraniak is regarded in Poland as a rival of Cardinal Wyszynski. That is plain nonsense. After all, he follows the Wyszynski line even more consistently than Wyszynski himself. The Curia and the Pope will never tolerate a disruption of the unity of the Polish bishops. This is the more so since they all, in the eyes of the Curia, are complete peers, no matter how different they may look to you. They are all chauvinistically patriotic. They all have one and the same axe to grind. They all display the same sympathetic attitude toward one and the same man and one and the same set of ideas in Poland. That represents for the Roman Curia such a paradox that it will never give preference to one Polish bishop over another, for it would have to fear that it has fallen victim to a mere nuance. You can be quite certain that the Curia wants nothing less than to split up the Polish episcopate into small splinter groups. Your presence here has served in a sense to assuage many of the Curia's worries. All those who have been here and, I suppose, those who are still going to come, manage to reconcile a paradoxical political line with perfect orthodoxy, an absolute lack of philosophical or social justification of their deeds with absolute submission in these matters to the relevant and binding views of the Church as they are manifest in its social theology."

"Even," I asked, "'when their way of acting and the binding views of the Church are at odds so that common sense fairly cries for some theory to clarify the contradiction?"

"Even then. The way your bishops are acting is right. One must act and not explain."

"Precisely," I said, "the way the Roman Curia and the Pope are in agreement with everything that is happening in Poland, accepting it even—supposedly—without any kind of *reservatio mentalis,* while simultaneously they manage to keep silent about it before the world and, in fact, to give false answers in this matter. What I have in mind is once again the prayer I mentioned, the radio address, and the *Osservatore*."

"Do those things really matter? Who reads them in your country? A few bishoprics and some monasteries are the only Polish subscribers to the *Osservatore*. And in those quarters the way all that must be read is fully understood."

"The bishoprics, the monasteries, *and* higher ministries. We here at the embassy, by the way, take another ten copies."

"That is definitely too much."

After this last exclamation he pondered for a while and added: "Neither you—despite everything that is said about you—are a dictatorship nor—despite everything that is said about us—are we. What has happened in your country between the state and the Church is a fact. It is a fact with which the Pope has not found fault. He has said so in the most authoritative way possible to the one man who has accepted the responsibility for this fact. You hold it against the Church that this was done only orally and not publicly and in writing. You are impatient. And I am not at all certain that you are fair toward the Church which finds itself at the turning point of one of the most difficult periods of its history. All of mankind and all of civilization does. There are periods in history during which the Church wins brilliant victories, but the grandeur of the achievement is in no way proportional to the tremendous dangers which threaten the Church. The result of our struggles with these dangers will prove crucially significant for the life and the very existence of the Church itself throughout the coming one hundred years. Do not imagine that it is only communism that beleaguers the Church in our days, and even when we speak of communism in particular we cannot mean European communism alone and especially not the communism of Poland. In any event—although at the present juncture in the continuity of our worries, this thing, in its significance for the world, does not resolve everything but just this much—the Church felt relief in taking cognizance of the new that has come into being in Poland. You find it amazing that the Church could not bring either itself or its organs of public communication to bear witness before the world to its genuinely felt response. But believe me, the Church is as little a dictatorship as you are one, regardless of what people say. In particular, it is no dictatorship when it has to reach a decision that runs counter to tradition, routine, customs, and habits. In such instances even the dictates of the Holy Father are weaker. Even those of Pius XII who speaks more authoritatively than many of his predecessors. His dictates grow weaker particularly when they run counter to his own habits and his own routine." [27]

This conversation clearly shows that Pius XII was quite aware of the fact that he lived at a turning point in history, that he recognized the changes that were underway, while he refused to say so. This attitude on the part of the Pope certainly contributed to the later deterioration in the relationship between the government and the episcopate in Poland. It simply is not compatible with the spirit of truthfulness which the prophets and Jesus of Nazareth represented when a man speaks in one way and thinks in another For, "Let your speech be, Yea, yea; Nay, nay." If a man consistently asks the servant girl every morning whether she is quite sure that she did not steal some silver spoons during the night, he will doubtless find after a few weeks that she really has stolen some in order to be able to say for once, Yea, yea. If one keeps telling the Polish communists that they do not amount to very much or again that they are no real communists (endangering through this latter statement their position within their group), they cannot be expected to consider this reaction a confirmation of the soundness of their course. Heads of state in this respect do not "stand above the situation" either. Their reactions are by and large just as naive as those of the man in the street.

Pius XII sensed himself to what extent he was unable to open up to the values of his time. He has a right to demand that his self-criticism and his last wishes be taken seriously. He wrote in his testament:

Lord, have mercy upon me, for Thy mercy is great.—These words, which I uttered at the moment when I agreed to my election to the position of the Highest Shepherd in full awareness of being unworthy and of not deserving it, I now repeat from a conviction that is the greater as my consciousness of the inadequacies, mistakes, and omissions that have occurred in the course of so long a pontificate during, to boot, so difficult and responsibility-laden an epoch have led my reason to understand still more clearly that I was unfit for and not equal to the role. Contritely I turn to all whom I may have wronged, whom I may

have treated unfairly or whom I injured by word or deed and ask their
forgiveness. I request those whose competence this request concerns that
they will not pay me great heed and make no plans for the erection of a
monument in my honor. Let it suffice that my poor mortal remains rest
undistinguished in a sacred place,—the less impressive a place the
better . . . [28]

The fact that the assertions and wishes of this Pope were not
taken seriously serves to show how little popes in general are
being taken seriously in Rome. For, if the last wishes a man utters
respecting his person are disregarded, all his other expressions
cannot possibly have fared any better.

Pius XII called himself unfit for his high office. If at the time
of his election the College of Cardinals included no better candi-
date, then this speaks unequivocally against the principle of selec-
tion that prevails in the Church. In any event, it was good that his
pontificate came to an end in 1958.

Owing to a slip—nothing more—Cardinal Roncalli became
Pope. The "caretaker Pope" John XXIII accomplished the decisive turn. Under him Catholic Christianity regained credibility.
He did not think highly of the condemnation of communism
but believed that the communists too can be spoken to in human
terms, just as the Orthodox, the Protestants, the Jews, the Mohammedans, and those of other faiths. To start a dialogue based
on mutual trust he offered deeds. He gave the green light for
opening the doors to the left for the Italian *democrazia chris-
tiana*. There followed his reception of Adzhubei. John accepted
the risk of an increase in the numbers of communist votes in
Italy as the price he had to pay in order to tackle the problem of
communism at its root.

It is in the light of this fundamental change that the Vatican's
new political course with respect to Poland must be seen. He
moved ahead in the direction of recognizing the Oder-Neisse line
in his now famous address to the Polish bishops during the Council session. He thus simultaneously met halfway the eastern demands for security, while—on the other hand—he contributed
his share to the international shock therapy which the politicians
of the Federal Republic of Germany appear to need. Today

certain positive response to that shock therapy is apparent, but in those days the patients in the Federal Republic were still ready to jump out of their skins. Through John XXIII the politics of reconciliation of the Catholics in the east (who were branded as traitors while Pius XII occupied the papal throne) came to be the official line—though no one thought it wise to say so in just those words—while the fight-minded politicians were dropped. To be sure the German ambassador to the Vatican was told that the address of the Pope to the Polish bishops was not meant to have quite the significance that was being read into it, but this could signify at worst that three steps ahead were followed by one step back. Such assuaging declarations represent only the chocolate coating of a pill which might otherwise be too bitter for the patient.

The Second Vatican Council began, and during the very first session the reactionaries suffered their first defeat. When Cardinal Wyszynski returned to Poland, he reported to Gomulka on what had happened at the Council.

The Polish government presented to the Sejm legislative bills which, both in school matters and in marriage questions, were highly problematic in terms of the desideratum of peace with the Catholic Church. To be sure, the separation of Church and state is a tenable point of view. But when religious instruction in the schools was abolished and the demand was made that from now on the Church would have to use its own facilities for the purpose, this clearly represented a breach of the "agreement of the government of the Republic of Poland with the Polish episcopate of April 14, 1950." The government countered with the reminder that the Church had likewise failed to fulfill its contractual obligations, especially in rural areas, with respect to the collectivization of agriculture. However, the Church had never been admonished in this matter. An Austrian politician, President Maleta of the National Council, asked in Warsaw in the Sejm why Polish agriculture had not also been collectivized and received the laconic reply: "The peasants do not want it." Was their reason for not wanting it that their priests did not want it? In any event, Polish agriculture has not fared too badly in its essentially Bukharinian course.

It would have been wiser to negotiate instead of acting unilaterally, but—all in all—one can recognize here a basis on which further work is possible.

Another highly problematic law is one permitting the interruption of pregnancies for social reasons. To be sure, in borderline cases in which the alternative is "death of the mother or death of the child," one cannot expect that non-Catholics will choose the death of the mother. But the legalization of abortions for "social" reasons represents an unnecessary provocation. The rejoinder that no one is forced under this law to interrupt a pregnancy and that no one is prevented by it from living according to Catholic precepts of ethics is quite justified, it is true, but in terms of Catholic morals such interventions still remain murder. Again, when Cardinal Wyszynski suggested that this law was reminiscent of the Nazi concentration camps, he surely went too far. It is a fact that the extremely high birth rate in Poland constitutes a very serious problem, but there are various approaches in the area of planned parenthood which do not have the same criminal character from the point of view of Catholic morality and which are not objected to by a number of other Christian churches.

Finally, we should mention in this connection that while it is true that the Polish clergy, in most instances, paid no taxes, the laws that were enacted to change this situation contained many features that were unnecessarily vexatious.

On the positive side, on the other hand, there is the fact that more than one thousand churches were restored or built anew. The construction of churches became possible in Yugoslavia only in 1966, in Czechoslovakia not even then.

The tension between the Polish government and the Church in Poland kept increasing. Meanwhile John XXIII died in Rome and Cardinal Montini from Milan was elected Pope as Paul VI. He does not have that all-pervading trust in God and in what is good in man that characterized his predecessor. He also had been for too long in the sphere of influence of Pius XII. After a short interlude of pushing further ahead, a phase of regression ensued. What went on in Rome during the last three Council sessions between the German and the Polish bishops and the refugees is not quite clear. It seems certain that a complicated process was set in motion which subsequently, in 1966, led to a grave crisis in Poland.

One faction of the Polish bishops, under the leadership of the Primate, proved in many ways extremely reactionary. We have noted before the opposition to the introduction of the vernacular into the liturgy. There was also evidence of an anti-ecumenical attitude, attributable—in its anti-Protestant aspect—to the fact that so many Germans are Protestants and—in its anti-Orthodox aspect—to the fact that Orthodoxy in this context meant primarily Russian Orthodoxy.

It was Cardinal Wyszynski who proposed that the Virgin Mary should officially be given the title of honor of "Mother of the Church." This incident played a role in the subsequent Czestochowa conflict which we shall have to discuss in greater detail. The antecedents of the conflict are as follows.

In 1960 all of Poland celebrated the five hundred and fiftieth anniversary of the Battle of Grünwald-Tannenberg that was fought in 1410 between the Teutonic Order and a Polish-Lithuanian army. The victory of the Poles entailed a decisive weakening of the Teutonic Order, this festering boil in the flank of the Catholic Church. Near Grünwald the grave of the then Grand Master of the Teutonic Order can still be seen. The Poles left the tombstone intact. Its inscription reads: "In this place Grand Master Ulrich von Jungingen died the death of a hero on July 15, 1410, fighting to the end for all that is German, for German law and order."

The Catholic Church of Poland celebrated with deep conviction the anniversary of the victory over this Cross-camouflaged horde of conquest-lusting gangsters. Cardinal Wyszynski, too, pointed to the pride which at that time rode before a fall. In the evaluation of this historical event there were no essential differences between the government and the episcopate.

In 1965 came another anniversary. Twenty years previously the territory held by Germany east of the Oder-Neisse line had been given to Poland. The wave of jubilation that swept through Poland on this occasion is readily understood if one considers the suffering inflicted on the Poles by the Germans. However, as we read the sermon which Cardinal Wyszynski preached on the subject, we cannot find his argumentation particularly convincing. He stated among other things that in the formerly German and now Polish areas "the very stones spoke Polish." I had occasion to hear a Russian Orthodox sermon in the Alexander Nevski Cathedral in Leningrad.[29] The priest said that it must be our endeavor to do God's will but that it was often difficult to know what God's will is. Whoever has been trying to do God's will cannot but agree with this statement. It seems, however, that Cardinal Wyszynski is convinced that he knows God's will. The Russian priest was more modest. The statement that "the very stones speak Polish" certainly goes too far. In Vienna there are Roman ruins under what is now the Hohe Markt, and similar ruins can be found in many places in Austria south of the Danube. These ruins consist of stones which "speak Latin." Yet, not even the most rabid amongst the Italian neo-fascists go so far as to demand that all territories with "Latin-speaking stones" must be "returned" to Italy.

It is high time that the Poles stop bolstering their claims to what now constitutes the western part of their country by historical arguments, although Pope John XXIII, too, used the expression, "territories recovered centuries later." The Polish claim to these lands can be justified much more directly. In the course of the past sixty years Germany waged two imperialistic wars. Surely, the war criminal Hitler—the "greatest genius of strategy of all time"—had worthy precursors: the war criminal Bismarck, alias "the iron chancellor," and the war criminal Friedrich II, aptly known as "the great" and lovingly referred to as "Alter Fritz," and also the eastward-expansive Teutonic Knights, all with criminally warlike inclinations.

After Hitler's attack on Poland, the Germans maltreated this people in such a fiendish way—abandoning them to hunger, condemning them to illiteracy, slaughtering them by the millions —that every decent German must feel in the depths of his heart the desire to show a modicum of good will and to atone at least in part, by relinquishing a portion of formerly German lands and by abandoning for the time being the objective of reunification, for the crimes that have been committed in the name of the

German people. Those who have been murdered cannot be brought back to life. Those who have died of hunger can no longer be fed.

For what has happened no counterclaims can be made. It is certainly true that during the expulsion of the Germans from the now Polish western territories instances occurred of similar crimes committed by Poles against innocent individuals. However, many of these Germans were not expelled at all; they fled before the advancing Russian armies. The Russians had no particular reason either to have friendly feelings toward the Germans. Remember the horror-inspiring cemeteries of 600,000 Leningraders, the farms burnt to the ground, the Russian prisoners that were murdered or allowed to starve to death. However regrettable individual Polish crimes may be, the ultimate reckoning will have to designate them as "excesses of self-defense," while the German crimes were not only committed on an incomparably larger scale but can only be designated as "premeditated murder." It is impossible to imagine a people capable in its totality and without exception of a sufficiently high degree of heroic Christianity to undergo for years the most cruel torture and to muster—after its ultimate liberation—the self-discipline of sparing its torturers.

There are neo-fascist papers in Germany whose collaborators knew how to dispose of all Christian-humane trends and endeavors by dubbing them "Jewish inferiority" (in the spirit of Goebbels's dictum: "Revenge is a dish that should be eaten cold") but which now demand leniency in the treatment of the Germans, accusing anyone of hatred who dares recall past German crimes. Christian charity is something the criminal may hope for on the part of the one he has harmed, but it is not something which he has a right to demand. For these reasons it is not more than fair that the Germans should abandon all claims to their formerly eastern territories. This view is shared by virtually all the neighbors of the Germans.

One need not be a friend of the German Democratic Republic to note that its attitude in these questions is not only more Christian but also more intelligent. It recognizes the two world wars as crimes instigated by Germany and recognizes the eastern

frontiers of Germany as they were fixed—all the denials to the
contrary notwithstanding—in 1945 in Potsdam. These facts should
suffice to assign to the German Democratic Republic an international role somewhat above the lowermost rung of the ladder.
From the Polish point of view the attitude of the German Democratic Republic is of the greatest importance.

A point imparting to the historical argumentation of the Poles
at least a certain justification is that Germany's eastward
expansion is a matter of historical continuity (from the Teutonic
Order to Hitler) which makes it difficult for the Poles to forget
the wrongs that were done them on so many occasions. When a
landowner has an expansion-craving neighbor who takes away
a piece of his holdings, he may eventually manage to forget and
accept the event. But if the neighbor takes another piece and still
another, the recollection of the first wrong will stay alive longer
than would have otherwise been the case.

In a certain way this comparison is applicable to the Polish-
Russian relations. It is often characteristic of nationalists (and
invariably of fascists) that they dream of erecting national empires restoring the maximum extension of their countries in the
past. Italian nationalists dream of the Roman Empire, their
French counterparts of the empire of the Franks or of Napo-
leon, the Spaniards of the empire of Charles V. The Polish
nationalists continue dreaming even today of the great Polish-
Lithuanian empire. Marshal Pilsudski marched in 1919 into the
Ukraine because he wanted to build once again a Greater
Poland. This reminded the Russians of the expansive tendencies
of Greater Poland.

The cession of formerly Polish eastern territories to Russia
with their replacement by formerly German lands in the west of
Poland, binds this country politically to the Soviet Union.

The Polish episcopate was outspoken in its endorsement of
the Polish western claims and was sorely chided for this attitude
by the press in the Federal Republic of Germany. The West-
German Catholics, who do not excell by a spirit of penitence with
respect to the monstrous deeds of the Third Reich, had little
understanding for the views of the Polish Primate. To be sure,
"Polish-speaking stones" belong in the category of nationalist-

chauvinist fantasy, but the basic acknowledgement that the formerly German territories were now legitimately Polish should have been endorsed by the West Germans.

The year 1966 was marked by the millennial celebration of the Christianization of Poland. It goes without saying that a people cannot be Christianized within a single year, but in those early days the baptism of whoever was king at the time meant in practice that the entire people had accepted the new religion. In 966 the Polish Duke Mieszko I was baptized. His motives—as must be expected in such cases—were doubtless complex, but it seems certain that his wife Dombrowka, the daughter of the Czech king, had exerted her influence in favor of baptism. It is this influence which the Polish bishops stressed in their invitation to the German bishops. One would have thought that in view of the Czech descent of Dombrowka the Czech bishops would be assigned a place of honor. Yet, the very opposite came to pass. The explanation for this fact must be looked for in the contempt which Cardinal Wyszynski and some of his Polish colleagues have for the Czech and Hungarian bishops. Cardinal Wyszynski considers himself a "resistance bishop," while he looks upon the Czech and Hungarian bishops as bishops of the regime. When the Polish government inquired why Wyszynski had failed to invite the Czech and Hungarian bishops, he insisted that he had presented the invitation to Cardinal Beran in Rome. It then transpired that indeed the Czech bishops had been invited, but only in a more or less casual way, not with the emphatic formality characteristic of the invitation extended to the German bishops. The information with which the Polish government was provided cannot, therefore, be regarded as complete. Official spokesmen of the Polish government kept emphasizing the national Polish motives underlying Mieszko's baptism. The event, seen in this light, marked the affiliation of Poland with the West.

The millennial celebration has various aspects: the concentration of the Church festivities in Czestochowa, the invitation sent to the Pope, the invitation of the German bishops, the invitation of the Spanish bishops, the initial cold-shouldering of the Czech and Hungarian and also the Russian-Orthodox dignitaries of the Church.

Because of the historical background, the millennial celebration —this must not be overlooked—was bound to have an anti-Russian undertone. Where Roman Catholicism ends Western civilization ends and the barbaric east begins . . . And all that sort of nonsense. Gomulka's endeavor to minimize these undercurrents could be successful only insofar as it had the sympathetic backing of the Church. It would seem that Paul VI did not fully grasp the implications of the problem. Indeed, it is a complex problem that is not easy to understand. Anti-Russian chauvinism is still widespread among the Poles and does not rank among the most lovable traits of this people. The true Christian spirit, as it was revived during the Second Vatican Council, should have meant in the case of Poland that the negative dregs of the people would not be stirred up but pumped out. Since thus the endeavor of the Polish government coincided with the dictates of Christian ethics, the Church should have given the government, in this matter, its unequivocal support. Indeed; it is time that the Poles stopped regarding themselves as something better than the Russians. But Cardinal Wyszynski exploited the nationalist-chauvinist attitude of wide circles for the purpose of anti-Russian agitation.

The focal point of all the celebrations of the millennium was Czestochowa. It will be recalled that Czestochowa played a special role in the defensive struggle against the Swedes. The historical event of the proclamation of the Virgin Mary as Queen of Poland inspired Cardinal Wyszynski to evolve a somehow mysticistic concept as a solution of the communist problem. His reasoning must have been something like this: In those days Czestochowa was besieged and most of Poland was occupied. Today the Church is besieged or occupied, and the occupying forces are the forces of communism. In those days the Swedes left as a result of the vow that the Virgin Mary would be proclaimed Queen of Poland. Today the communists will "leave" if the Virgin Mary is proclaimed "Mother of the Church." On the basis of such reflections, Cardinal Wyszynski began to insist in Rome that the new title be made official. Cardinal Suenen remarked wittily: "That makes Mary our grandmother, for the Church is our mother." This annoyed Cardinal Wyszynski no end.

The vast majority of the bishops did not wish to have this new title conferred on Mary. Their motives were primarily a matter of ecumenical tact. After all, Mary does have quite a series of titles, as anyone interested can see from the Litany of Loretto. The idea that Mary might be interested in additional titles is clearly a naive projection to the Mother of God of subjective ambitions of clerical career-seekers, for the gospels show that Mary at all times gave God the honor. It may be assumed that she would rejoice incomparably more at seeing suppressed and exploited peoples helped to an existence more in keeping with human dignity than at receiving additional honorific titles. (Though I cannot resist at this point recalling that during the First World War the Italian Medal for Bravery was conferred upon Mary, an incident that induced Karl Kraus to move a step farther away from the Church.)

However, Cardinal Wyszynski's Mariology has in addition a markedly political background. A considerable number of Polish emigrants, who represent in Rome a fairly important pressure group, is of the opinion that Cardinal Wyszynski must be regarded as the real political authority in Poland, with the implication that the generally recognized Polish government is merely a puppet of the Soviet Union. That, to say the least, is a slight exaggeration, for after the Polish October of 1956 there were legally valid elections.

The titles of Mary include also that of *Magna Mater Austriae*. But no one in Austria sees in this more than a pious and amiable metaphor, and no one would think of claiming this title of Mary's to be replete with political implications. Neither conservative nor socialist politicians have the feeling that it imposes any kind of restraint on their rights and obligations. At best, Catholic polititians may feel on occasion that Mary's being the Mother of Austria represents for them an additional obligation to be honest in their political endeavors.

In the thinking of Cardinal Wyszynski the rule of Mary over Poland is something incomparably more real. The "true" rulership of Mary contrasts with the "false" or "untrue" rulership of Gomulka and his comrades. Now, no Catholic and no member of an Orthodox Church will hesitate for a moment to admit that Mary would rule Poland (or any other country) better than Gomulka (or any other politician). There is, however, a hitch in all this. So far Mary has never ruled anywhere in person, no matter how many titles of rulership have been conferred upon her. And that is where the delicate problem of the vicarship begins. Who is Mary's vicar?

In fact, Mary has never designated anyone as her official representative. No one has ever been in possession of an authentic accreditation by Mary. Yet, Cardinal Wyszynski appears to favor the thesis that he is the appointed representative of Mary, though we are still waiting for tangible proofs in this matter. Is he really quite certain that Mary—being *Magna Mater Austriae*—would prefer Cardinal König as the deciding political power in Austria? It is just as uncertain that she would prefer to see Cardinal Wyszynski rather than Gomulka as the head of state in Poland. One should not imagine that the heavenly powers are invariably siding with the Catholics.

It can hardly be claimed that the gospel provides sufficient information on the political ideas of Mary to make it possible to rule Poland on the basis of principles endorsed by her. Still, the little there is supports certain decisive inferences with respect to her basic political concepts. In her grandiose *Magnificat* which—even though it is perhaps not fully authentic—does appear to reflect her principles, there is an enthusiastic glorification of God with the lines:

> He scatters those proud in the fancy of their hearts.
> He puts down princes from their thrones.
> And exalts those of low degree.
> The hungry He fills with good things;
> And the rich He sends away empty-handed.[30]

Whether Cardinal Wyszynski in his traditionally conservative basic attitudes upholds this revolutionary philosophy is more than questionable, and the doubt one may have about his being the most fully qualified representative of Mary would not appear to be wholly unjustified.

Pope Paul VI—in one of his interventions in the goings-on at the Vatican Council (of which to date not one has proved wise)—did appoint Mary "Mother of the Church." Thereupon Cardinal Wyszynski returned to Poland, his chest swollen with pride. In reality, the title has so far met with little favor within the Church. What determined Paul VI, one wonders, to go through with this conferral? He must have known of Cardinal Wyszynski's mechanistic concept of heavenly operations according to which Mary responds to the conferral of a new title by chasing the communists away. It is quite in keeping with a basic character trait of the Pope that he should tend to impart to the simplest things a mysticistic sheen. Michael Serafian wrote in this connection:

There is in Paul's character a vital desire to achieve schematic clarity, intellectual formulation, concise outlines, and neatly defined limits which he will never cross or even approach but which he will never lose sight of. To be sure, this kind of "schematicism" does not fully satisfy his spirit, for he realizes the many dangers inherent in such an intellectual pinning down of outlines and confines: He who is inclined in this direction will easily fall victim to the familiar weakness of the intellectual to think of words as deeds. For this reason Paul's mentality is balanced, as it were, by a mystical side, a constant urge to veil intellectual formulations and theoretical postulates by an animating hue of mysticism, to attenuate the underlying rigidity, or to take inspiration as a substitute for concrete actions which his words by themselves cannot bring about. When we use the term mysticism with reference to Paul VI, we are not speaking of the kind of spiritual mysticism we instinctively associate with the names of St. Theresa of Avila or of St. John of the Cross. Much less do we intend to allude to the literary style and the terminology of Paul VI. He does prefer Italianizing turns of expression such as *disegno immenso e misterioso; arcanum consilium; celsissimum finem; mysterium novi temporis; consilium inscrutabile* [infinite and mysterious design; secret counsel; highest goal; secret of the new age; inscrutable wisdom]. But that is not the mysticism of which we are here speaking.

He avoids insofar as possible crass formulations of hard truths and seems to strive—doubtless for the benefit of his own mentality as well as of that of others—to invest all formulations with a delicately otherworldly, transmaterial, and impersonal coating. At times, however, he is quite capable of using expressions that have the lash of a whip. In case of extreme necessity he will always be able to withdraw behind the protective wall of mysticism. He finds his position threatened only when there is no mystic cover that can blur the schematic outline of his thought. As a prerequisite of smoothly functioning continuities he requires the theoretical and the practical side of things, but both are imbued with his inner mysticism. [31]

It may well be that it was this aspect of his character that moved Paul VI to give in to the urgings of Cardinal Wyszynski. After a sleepless night he announced, against the wishes of the majority of the bishops, that he had decided in favor of conferring the new title on Mary. In the thought patterns of Cardinal Wyszynski the Pope is the "true" ruler of the world, and only the deceptive wiles of Satan prevent men from recognizing this fact.

Paul VI went on spinning his yarn of Mariological mysticism. John XXIII had seriously propagated throughout the Catholic world the idea of peace (even with respect to the communists), specifically in his encyclical *Pacem ın terris.* This document was addressed to "all men of good will" (in the words of the Evangelical Christmas tidings). John was ready to look for this "good will" in men of the most varied faiths and philosophies of life and to recognize it wherever it was found. If one's endeavor is to establish a dialogue with all men thus qualified, one must carefully see to it that the basis of one's arguments is not specifically Catholic. It would not be fair to suggest Catholic theses with respect to the question of peace to honest men and women who are not Catholics. There is much in *Pacem in terris* that is objectionable, but all in all this encyclical does represent a remarkable attempt. Paul VI, doubtless with the best intentions, continued the peace work of his predecessor. He visited the United Nations Headquarters, he became involved in Viet Nam, and he initiated various other moves. Yet, his peace encyclical of 1966 dealt with the "Queen of the Rosary," who, after all, is a concept only to Catholics.

The subliminal political significance associated with the name of Czestochowa as well as Cardinal Wyszynski's endeavor to utilize—on a lend-lease basis, as it were—Poland's past in the interest of Catholicism on the occasion of the millennial celebration could only serve to emphasize the conflict. With a little good will on both sides it should have been possible—perhaps by means of a progressive Catholic pastoral letter—to arrive at a joint declaration. The Polish episcopate wanted the Pope to visit Cze-stochowa. That was, indeed, in the interest of the Vatican, for all other possible destinations for a papal journey would have led to misinterpretations. Had he gone only to Warsaw, the implication would have been an insult to Czestochowa, the "spiritual capital" of Poland. Had he gone to Cracow and Warsaw, with possibly a detour to Czestochowa to celebrate a mass without a sermon, certain German circles would have tried to read all sorts of interpretations into the fact that the Pope's journey did not take him through formerly German territory. Had Paul VI gone in addition to Gdansk, Poznan, and Wroclaw, that would have been grist for the mills of the West German refugee organizations. Only Czestochowa was, from the point of view of non-Polish observers, of "purely religious" significance. However, the Polish government feared a political demonstration on the part of Cardinal Wyszynski. To be sure, Paul VI and Czestochowa could have functioned as a peacemaker between the German and Polish cardinals, but the event would have served to strengthen the authority of Cardinal Wyszynski more than a little.

Had the Pope visited Poland, he would have had to distinguish Poland in some way, preferably by appointing two cardinals. Poland has approximately thirty million Catholics. It is true, in the appointment of cardinals the Church is not always guided by the number of Catholics residing in a particular country, but if Austria with its seven million Catholics has one cardinal, while Germany with its twenty-five million Catholics has four, it seems but fair that Poland should have at least three.

It would be unfair to insinuate that the Vatican meant to slight Poland. Its restraint is, paradoxically, once again attributable to Cardinal Wyszynski. Although this man is an extreme Polish nationalist, he objects to the appointment of new Polish cardinals. The reason is his desire to rule alone. It is difficult for a man of his conservative bend of mind to admit that the Holy Ghost might bestow its blessings not only on him but on others as well. The Cardinal, furthermore, thinks—and in this he is not entirely wrong—that one or two additional cardinals in a Polish conference of bishops might form a majority against him. Such an eventuality would suit the Polish government. The result of all this is that in Poland the communists would like to see several cardinals, while the nationalistic cardinal who is there does not wish to have a peer.

It is quite true, traditionally there are in Poland two cardinal's sees: Cracow and Wroclaw. There are several reasons to account for the fact that the government would not like to see a cardinal in Cracow. This city is the center of conservativism in Poland. The contrast between Cracow, the old royal residence where the last of those dreaming of Emperor Francis Joseph I have not yet died, and modern Warsaw is very much the same as the contrast between Byzantium and Moscow in the world of the eastern churches. It is the contrast between an old aristocrat and an upstart. To blunt the spearpoint of Krakau, the town of Nowa Huta was founded in 1945 in its vicinity. The center of Nowa Huta was built in Stalinist classicism, but the buildings erected since 1956 are remarkably modern.

If Wroclaw were again to become a cardinal's see, the implication would naturally be a further step toward the recognition of the Oder-Neisse line. It is for this reason that the Polish government might even put up with a cardinal in Cracow. It is likely that the envoy of the Federal Republic of Germany would file a note of complaint with the Cardinal Secretary of State at the Vatican, merely to be told with an undertone of amazed innocence that "nothing had happened" and that the international press "misinterpreted this measure," imputing "wholly irrelevant motives to a decision of purely religious significance," that it was "totally incomprehensible how such wrong inferences could be arrived at in view of the fact that the Vatican had never . . . ," and similar quotations from the dictionary of standard phrases for the dismissal of inopportune diplomats. In this respect German diplomacy is hopelessly inferior to that of the Vatican.

In the event of a papal visit to Czestochowa the appointment of two new Polish cardinals would have been practically unavoidable. Paul VI, after all, would have had to offer his hosts a "little something" in recognition of their hospitality. To be sure, Paul VI could have gone further. If he had wanted to stress the shared interests of the Vatican, the Polish government, and the Soviet Union against the type of Polish nationalism represented by Cardinal Wyszynski, he could have said that he had come as a "herald of peace" and "messenger of love" and that "he was happy that two nations as important and estimable as the Poles and the Russians" were now living "in shared peace" and had found their way "to an attitude of mutual respect." However, it is questionable whether Paul VI would have spoken in this vein, for in doing so he would have made clear to the Polish clergy and to large segments of the Polish population that the Pope was pulling the rug from under the feet of the Cardinal. Such utterances would have represented the maximum possible of a relatively public disavowal.

The appointment of new Polish cardinals is not a new project, but all past attempts in this direction were vetoed by Cardinal Wyszynski. To be sure, the Vatican could simply impose is authority, but it wishes to pay tribute to the decentralizing tendencies of the Second Vatican Council. After the conclusion of the fourth session, Archbishop Kominek did not return directly to Wroclaw but underwent in Austria a course of medical treatments and stayed on in Vienna to the end of January of the following year. The appointment of fifty new cardinals was expected, but the implementation of the plan was postponed.

This raises the question as to why the appointment of all the cardinals and not just that of the Polish cardinals was postponed. It seems certain that Cardinal Wyszynski's arguments had included the point that the Polish state would profit from the appointment of new cardinals in terms of the axiom of *divide et impera*. It may be assumed that the Vatican was determined to overrule his objections and decided to exert moral pressure on him by withholding the appointment of all the other cardinals as well. The logic of it must have been something like this: Fine, there will be no appointments of Polish cardinals, but there will be no appointments of other cardinals either. Obviously, Archbishop Kominek knows—as do all the other bishops that were about to be raised to the status of cardinals—that it is only the veto of Cardinal Wyszynski that prevents the Vatican from proceeding with its plan. It is quite likely that none of these bishops will, as a result, love Cardinal Wyszynski the more passionately, but it is not likely that any of them will give the Cardinal an inkling of what he really feels. Still, the Cardinal is no fool, and he is bound to sense the reaction of the others. This will of necessity subject him to some form of moral pressure.—Insofar as Cardinal Wyszynski did experience such pressure, he responded to it by becoming still more aggressive.

Finally—after two visits to Poland by Undersecretary of State Casaroli (to which we shall have to refer once again in another context)—Paul VI did appoint new cardinals in 1967. As a past master of the combination of "both this and that" with "neither this nor that," he appointed—contrary to the wishes of Cardinal Wyszynski—among others also a Polish cardinal. That he appointed only one paid heed to the wishes of the Polish government. That he appointed the Cardinal of Cracow and not the Cardinal of Wroclaw was contrary to the government's wishes. Yet, all in all, the appointment was more in keeping with the interests of the government than with the purposes of Cardinal Wyszynski.

In the conflict between state and Church in Poland, a certain importance must be attributed, furthermore, to a Polish refugee and his work. Oscar Halecki holds a professorship at the Pilsudski Institute in New York. The very name of this Institute permits inferences as to the person of Halecki. Marshal Pilsudski—as mentioned before—was intent upon establishing a new Greater Poland. And Halecki is likewise of the opinion that the Baltic and the Black Sea are Poland's "natural boundaries." He alludes to this fact in his standard short history of Poland.

If one insists on applying this historical image to the present situation, one must conclude that the Poles cannot but reclaim their eastern territories. This would represent a provocation to any government of the Soviet Union, as it would have been and as it was once for a bourgeois liberal or even a feudal Russian government. Obviously, no Polish government can identify itself with such principles. "Natural boundaries" are always a highly questionable concept, particularly so in the case of Poland where there is nothing boundarywise but the Baltic in the North and the Carpathians in the South. Halecki's name figured twice in the affair: Once when the Polish bishops enclosed a copy of Halecki's book with their invitation to the German bishops and again when Halecki was proposed as the main speaker for the occasion of the great millennial celebration in Rome. The idea underlying the gift of the book to the German bishops was obviously to suggest that the bishops would do well to familiarize themselves somewhat with Poland's history. It is, as such, a sound idea, but it is doubtful whether familiarity with Poland's history can be achieved to the desirable extent by means of Halecki's book. When in the course of the subsequent discussion regarding the letter of invitation the Polish bishops were asked about the Halecki aspect, Archbishop Kominek replied that what had been involved was the manuscript of a new book by Halecki that had not as yet appeared in print. It was, in fact, a German translation of the aforementioned history of Poland which was first published in London in Polish. This Polish version contained a chapter that was omitted when the book appeared in the German translation. In this chapter the liberation of Poland from communism was predicted as coinciding with the millennial celebration. The reason is probably that 1000 is such a nice round figure.

It was at the invitation of Cardinal Wyszynski that Professor Halecki was to speak in Rome on the occasion of the millennial celebration. When the cardinal applied for a passport to go himself to Rome, his application was turned down. At this time, however, the whole affair was approaching its critical climax. The point at issue was specifically the letter of invitation to the German bishops. It seems likely that there had been negotiations between the Polish and the German bishops on this score during the Council sessions in Rome. No details regarding this matter are known, but it does not seem that the proceedings were handled with outstanding diplomatic skill. In particular, the political intelligence of the German bishops should never be overrated, although it is probable that they had asked for advice from the German Foreign Office.

The Polish bishops had certainly been guilty of a gross breach of political protocol, particularly in view of the tenseness of the situation prevailing in the area of foreign affairs between Poland

and the Federal Republic of Germany. Their excuse that there was no law obligating them to consult the Polish Foreign Office is technically quite sound, but they should have foreseen that the way they went about it was bound to rub the Foreign Office and the government the wrong way and that any other Foreign Office and any other government would have shown the same reaction. Shortly before the transmittal of the letter, the Polish ambassador in Rome had given a reception for the Polish bishops, but even that was let go by without a word concerning the invitation. At least a little good will, a token of readiness to cooperate with the government would have been called for.

However, a point still weightier in the eyes of a Christian layman (or, better, of a secular Christian) is the incredible disregard for the Catholic groups—the Znak, Pax, and the Christian-Social Society—in the Sejm, the Polish parliment. The Znak is supposed to be in the confidence of Cardinal Wyszynski. For that reason, the two other groups are not associated to the same extent with the cardinal's intentions, and the cardinal's actions do not affect their reputation in a favorable or unfavorable way. If in so complicated a situation the politicians were to act in support of the cardinal's objectives, it was not more than a demand of the most elementary fairness that a matter as weighty as the letter of invitation should have been discussed with the groups referred to. Yet, the reactions of those groups show that the fact of that letter took them as much by surprise as it did the government. Indeed, it takes more than a modicum of feudalistic Führer-ism to expect responsible politicians to abide by the wishes of the bishops without being given the possibility of expressing their views. This type of lord-and-master attitude on the part of bishops ought to have been a matter of the past after the Second Vatican Council. The Znak had no choice but to dissociate itself from the letter, and it did so not without bitterness.

The reaction of the Polish authorities would doubtless have been different if the German bishops had shown greater courage. That the Polish and the German bishops should differ in their attitudes toward the communists is easily understood because they differ in the historical background of their thinking, but it is less easy to find an excuse for the fact that there were also a number

of behavioral slips—to put it charitably—relative to the new ecu-
menicalism. This is apparent, for instance, from the extremely
restrained document, "Standpoint of the Polish Ecumenical Council." All in all, however, the neutral outsider reading this release
cannot but have the impression that it is replete with good will to
the point of naiveté. The German press, with its often devious
insinuations, did not help matters any. The basic tendency of the
document is certainly conciliatory, and this—in view of the shame-
ful demeanor of the German occupation in Poland—must be
recognized as proof of magnanimity and broad-mindedness. The
formula "forgive and ask forgiveness" in the second to last paragraph epitomizes the document's conciliatory spirit. There was
reason enough for the German bishops to make every effort to
show themselves worthy of that spirit.

The commandment that we should forgive our enemies is not
always easy to understand for a Christian. A communist is bound
to find it still harder, if not impossible, to understand. A preparatory attempt to explain matters might have been useful. In any
event, it is proof of the broad-mindedness of the Polish bishops
that they referred approvingly to German bishops, such as Faul-
haber, who—in fact—had never condemned the attack on Poland
although he had come out against Nazism. It was equally broad-
minded to make mention of the German resistance fighters whose
numbers were infinitesimally small in comparison with the over-
whelming majority of German collaborators in Hitler's crimes,
that is, the whole Wehrmacht and all the members of the home-
front organizations. The German bishops were thus well advised
when they spoke in their reply of the Polish "magnanimity"
that had induced the writers of the document "to mention first
and foremost, from among all the events that had occurred down
through the centuries, instances accruing to the honor of
your people and ours." This sentence is not quite logical. The
words "of your people" should have been omitted, for it is not
magnanimous to mention events accruing to one's own honor
(particularly if there are so few of them). If the Germans failed
to prove themselves worthy of the Polish magnanimity, they
alone bear the blame.

Was it the intent of the Polish bishops to bring up for debate the question of the Oder-Neisse line? Both Polish and German spokesmen of the press have claimed that this was so. Later on Gomulka tried to minimize the point. In any event, there is at least one sentence in the Polish letter of invitation that establishes the finality of the Oder-Neisse border. This border is referred to as a most important problem, "a hot iron." The words that follow need to be carefully analyzed in all their implications: "The Western frontier of Poland along the Oder and Neisse rivers is for Germany, as we fully understand, an extremely bitter fruit of the last war of massive destruction." What is this meant to mean? "The frontier is a fruit." That statement is fully clear to those who read it without prejudice. That the fruit is called "bitter," shows understanding and a certain broad-mindedness. To be sure, one might reproach the Polish bishops with having over-rated German sensitivity and German tact. There are people who won't understand what is not impressed upon them with a sledgehammer, for they are lacking the subtler organs that are needed to comprehend nuances of language.

It was quite unnecessary to disclaim the decisions of the Potsdam Conference of 1945. After all, not only the Poles but the Russians, too, had borne their full measure of hardship and horror. (There were six hundred thousand dead at Leningrad alone.) Since the Russo-German border was anyway quite short, it made utter sense to adjust the western limits not only of Poland but of the Soviet Union as well. The Poles got the better deal. It would have been unwise for the Poles to come to an understanding with the Germans at the expense of the Russians. The Germans ought to have been told simultaneously about the injustice toward the Russians. The German-Polish relations cannot be normalized if the Polish-Russian and the German Russian relations are not clarified at the same time. I quite intentionally say "Russian" rather than "Soviet," for what is involved is only to a very minor extent a matter of relations with the Soviet communists but rather a matter of relations to the Russians and Ukrainians.

The Polish bishops referred in the matter of the Oder-Neisse line to the Potsdam decisions of the great powers, that is, the "victorious power" (of which Poland cannot be claimed to be one). The way the borderlines are drawn in eastern Europe

goes back above all to the demands of the Soviet Union. The
Polish bishops do not recognize the justification of these demands
and hence do not recognize the justification of the borders. They
declared, as it were, their innocence and referred the Germans
to the Russians instead of emphasizing their solidarity with
the Russians. This raises simultaneously the question of the thesis
of the "conquered" Poland. It is based on the assumption
that Poland was first defeated by the Germans and then by the
Soviets. To be sure, the Soviets favored a communist rule in Poland, but they did not try to extinguish the Poles as a nation. It
was not their endeavor to russify the Poles. In their attitudes
toward the Germans, Poles and Russians—apart from the Jews—
ought to be united in solidarity, for they were the principal
victims of the last war.

Although the Polish bishops referred to the Oder-Neisse line
as a "fruit" of the Second World War and thus acknowledged it to
be definitive, the eternally yesterday-minded among the Germans
derived hope from the reserved attitude of the Polish bishops
toward the Russians, implying that it might be possible to negotiate with them relative to the Oder-Neisse line once the question
of the western borders of Russia could be made the subject of
negotiations with the Russians (or the object of a power struggle
with them). In West Germany the idea was widely held that it
would be possible to enter into an alliance with the Polish
bishops and the conservative Catholics of Poland against the
Russians, while the Polish communists would side with the Russians against the West Germans. There are in the letter of invitation of the Polish bishops various passages which prove that it
was not the intention of the bishops to promote anti-Russian
and anti-communist feelings. A case in point is the fact that they
mentioned Paulus Wlodkowicz who spoke up at the Council of
Constance for the right of the heathens to be heathen. This mention represented not only an attack against the Teutonic Order
but implied also a criticism of the methods by which Greater
Poland had tried to Catholicize and Latinize the Russian Orthodox. In order to understand this criticism, a little more historical
awareness of the events in Greater Poland is needed than most
Germans can claim to have. The further mention in the letter of

St. Andrew Bobola, S.J., who had been slain by the Cossacks because of his stubborn struggle against an independent Ukraine, shows the entire ambivalence of the attitude of the Polish bishops.

Finally—and this represents surely at the same time a concession to the Polish state and the Soviet Union—the Polish bishops stated in their letter: "Thousands of Germans shared as Christians and communists the fate of our Polish brethren in the concentration camps." (Nota bene, for background: The Communist Party in the Federal Republic of Germany has been outlawed. Illegal membership in it is severely punished, while former Nazis are being treated with kid gloves.) This observation did not sit too well with the Christian Democratic Union which is of the opinion that there was nothing wrong about locking up communists in concentration camps. After all, communists are being locked up today, too. For this reason the reference to the communists was regarded as pious hypocrisy on the part of the Polish bishops, as a concession to the state that did not deserve to be taken seriously. Yet, in contrast to this interpretation, it is highly probable that the Polish bishops were indeed convinced that the rounding up of communists in concentration camps was a grave injustice. It even seems possible to proceed in the interpretation of the text to the point of seeing in the reference to the communists a veiled reference to the German Democratic Republic whose existence was not otherwise alluded to anywhere.

The existence of the German Democratic Republic is of prime importance from the point of view of the security needs of the Soviet Union, Poland, and Czechoslovakia, but also of those of the other communist countries. No politician in any of these states could think of abandoning the German Democratic Republic to the Federal Republic of Germany, even if he were ready to disregard the dictates of his sense of loyalty toward the leaders of the East German people's democracy. Then, too, the western boundaries of Poland have been officially recognized by the German Democratic Republic. This point is of crucial importance to the Poles even if there are many matters in which they do not see eye to eye with the communists in the German Democratic Republic. More than one appraisal of that state is possible, but its position in the matter here under discussion can only be regarded as exemplary. A hint in that direction would have been no more than an expression of due appreciation.

The West German rejection, not to say denial, of the existence of the German Democratic Republic gave many West Germans the idea that the Polish bishops were ready to subscribe to the principles of political con-manship underlying the so-called Hallstein Doctrine. According to this doctrine the Federal Republic of Germany forbids all other states, under penalty of punitive sanctions, to recognize the German Democratic Republic. Many Federal Germans—including the Foreign Minister, the Chancellor, and Hallstein himself—have meanwhile come to realize that this product of diplomatic tomfoolery has no future. That is why "trade missions" with consular prerogatives are being set up in the eastern states. They are in fact embassies in disguise, but by not calling them that the fiction is maintained that Germany's foreign policies are characterized by a consistent continuity which in truth does not exist.

In spite of everything, the reaction of the Polish government to the invitation by the Polish bishops would certainly have been different if the German bishops in their reply had shown more diplomacy. Here the Catholic bishops of Germany might have been well advised to learn a lesson from the memorial issued by the Protestant churches. I refer to the "EKD" memorial of the Evangelical Churches in Germany. One must bear in mind in this connection that the leadership of the Protestants in Germany is superior to that of the Catholics. This goes back to the fact that after 1945 the two churches assumed different attitudes toward the men in leading positions who had failed during the Nazi era.

In the Protestant churches, too, leading churchmen had collaborated with the National-Socialist regime. Opposed to them was the "confessing church" with men like Niemöller, Bonhoeffer, Karl Barth, and others. After the collapse of the Nazi regime the church leadership that had been at Hitler's beck and call was relieved of its duties, and men were installed whose opposition to National Socialism could not be doubted. The Catholic episcopate, on the other hand, underwent no reshuffling.

In France the situation was basically different. De Gaulle insisted on purging the episcopate of collaborators. General De

Gaulle is a conscious Catholic with civilian courage and moral backbone. At the time of his visit in the Soviet Union he did nothing to veil the fact of his Catholic convictions. His endeavor to get certain bishops purged was hence in no way inspired by anti-Catholic motives. It is true, the Papal Legate Angelo Roncalli succeeded in the course of persistent negotiations in markedly reducing the number of bishops that were to be removed. Subsequently the French cardinals, who included several whom De Gaulle had had on his black list, showed their appreciation by working for Roncalli's election to the papal throne.

It is interesting to note that after 1945 no German and no Austrian Catholic bishop was relieved of his duties. There was only one instance where the position of an Austrian bishop seemed shaky for a while as a result of the fact that this man had supported the Nazis somewhat too energetically after the victory of the Allies. Catholic soul-searching was relatively slow in coming. It began only under the influence of Gordon Zahn's books, "German Catholicism and Hitler's Wars" [*Der deutsche Katholizismus und Hitlers Kriege*] and "Life and Death of Franz Jägerstätter" [*Das Leben und Sterben des Franz Jägerstätter*], and of Hochhuth's drama "The Deputy" [*Der Stellvertreter*]. This accounts for the fact that the German bishops do not sense the gravity of the crimes of the Nazis to the same extent as their Protestant counterparts and that they are less aware of the necessity that penance must be done by the Germans for the Nazi crimes. In the light of these facts it is no longer surprising that, compared to the EKD memorial, the answer the Catholic bishops of Germany addressed to the Polish bishops was morally weaker.

There is, on the other hand, no denying that the Catholic answer was not without positive elements. If we bear in mind to what extent the German clergy is accustomed to assuming an attitude of deferential obedience toward the state, we are inclined to note even a minor deviation from the official policies as a point of major significance. The zeal with which the document speaks of "Christian Europe" is, to be sure, somewhat suspicious, but fortunately there is no reference to the "Christian Occident" that might be opposed to the (un-Christian[?]) Orient. But there fol-

lows a passage in which the German guilt toward Poland is unequivocally admitted. The fact that the Polish gesture of asking
forgiveness is not mentioned accrues to the honor of the German
bishops, for the Polish guilt is such that it must be regarded as
hardly worth mentioning compared to the German guilt. A
further noteworthy point is that the German bishops expressly
acknowledge the Polish magnanimity of having mentioned German resistance which, after all, had never amounted to very
much.

There are in the answer of the German bishops three passages
that might be referred to in connection with the question of the
recognition of the Oder-Neisse border. After having stated that
terrible things had been done to the Poles by the Germans, the
bishops went on to say: "We know that we must bear the consequences of the war which are a heavy burden for our country,
too." What does this mean? If the demand for a restoration of the
borders of 1937 is satisfied, there is little by way of consequences
of the war the Germans have to bear. There follows this significant
passage: "We know well what these territories mean therefore to
present-day Poland. For this reason we must say to them in love
and truthfulness: If these Germans speak of their 'right to their
homeland,' this entails—with few exceptions—no aggressive intent. Our Silesians, Pomeranians, and East Prussians wish to
imply that they lived rightfully in their homelands and that they
remain bound to their homelands." If the bishops meant to
express in this way their conviction that the displaced are to return to their homelands, then the sentence would have had to
read: ". . . lived rightfully in their old homelands and will have
to live there rightfully again." But they only said "that they remain bound to their homelands." An emigrant, too, can remain
bound to his old home, such as the Polish-, Swedish-, and Hun-
garian-Americans who continue in their new country to wear
their old folk costumes and to practice their old folksongs and
folk dances. If the German bishops meant to say no more than
this, the next following sentence becomes incomprehensible: "And
so it [Christian charity] will help to overcome all the baleful
consequences of the war through a solution satisfactory in all
respects." Is the present border no satisfactory solution from the

German point of view? Do the Germans have a right to a "satisfactory" solution after this terrible war?

There appears to be a contradiction here. In trying to resolve
it we may think of three possible interpretations of the passage:

1. The Germans lived in the areas beyond the Oder-Neisse line
   and are to return there. The Poles are to return to the areas
   which now belong to the Soviets.
2. Germans and Poles are to live together in the formerly German eastern areas.
3. The Germans remain where they are and continue to practice
   the customs of their old homeland.

The last interpretation was utilized by the Polish bishops in
their defense against the reproaches of their government. The
second interpretation was that chosen by the government, thinking no doubt of Adenauer's plan of Poles and Germans living
together. The first interpretation was that chosen by the various organizations of displaced Germans.

In reality, however, the German bishops did not want to say
anything at all but to keep all roads open. This is an art of diplomacy in which bishops who have had to read repeatedly
the encyclicals of Pius XII have had excellent training. Everybody was free to read into and out of the text what he pleased. He
could replace any "if" by a "but," any "as well" by an "and also."
It may, nonetheless, be assumed that the bishops are inclined to
favor the third thesis. It is true, the members of the German episcopate do not, on the whole, exceed in their political skill the
typical education product of the German university, but it appears that finally even the German intellectuals have come to
suspect that a revision of the Oder-Neisse border is not wanted by
all other countries. Except in election campaigns, where the endeavor is to get the votes of the displaced for a particular party,
it thus has ceased to be meaningful to cling to the demand for
an Oder-Neisse revision. It seems that there are individuals in
the German government who continue to think that "reunification" might be bought for the price of recognizing the Oder-
Neisse line. But this illusion likewise begins to wane. The Ger-

man bishops could have been of great help to their Polish confreres by recognizing the Oder-Neisse border, but this might have brought down upon them the wrath of a handful of illusionist German politicians. That is why they preferred to limit themselves to a meaningless phrase.

Finally the German bishops noted that "the brotherhood of good will" could "derive courage from the [Vatican] Council . . . At the Council too, the course to be followed was not always clear. The goal was not always shining in unmistakable clarity . . . , but then, through God's grace, the way was shown and at times a surprising solution was given." This comparison with the Council signifies that the German bishops at present know nothing at all. The goal is unclear, the road leading to it is unknown, and a surprising solution through God's grace is expected. The Polish bishops in their letter addressed greetings to their Protestant brothers in Germany. This was a delicate reference to the EKD memorial. But the German bishops played deaf and waited for a surprising idea. In the long run, this surprising solution may be expected to be no more than that the Germans and the Poles remain where they are. As the situation is at present, this—however—will require to no small extent the intervention of God's grace.

It may be assumed with a high degree of certainty that the Vatican is quite aware of the immutability of the Polish-German border. There have been numerous hints to this effect, and John XXIII said so clearly and unequivocally. There is the hope that the Germans too will sooner or later become aware of this fact. A well-known Vatican official explained to me: "Were I—of course I won't—to state publicly that not even the Pope desires the reunification of Germany, I would expose myself to great unpleasantnesses."

The Polish government started a campaign against the Polish-German episcopal correspondence. In some respects that campaign was quite justified:

> The Polish bishops utilized in the endeavor to "enlighten" the German bishops a book by Halecki, and—indeed—they (or Cardinal Wyszynski alone) went so far as to invite Halecki to come to Rome to present a lecture.

They failed to inform the Polish Foreign Office of the planned correspondence. They did explain—though not clearly enough for those intent upon thinking otherwise—that they regarded the Polish western border to be definitive.

They failed in their communication to mention the German Democratic Republic.

A point of significance in connection with this correspondence is, furthermore, that the bishops spoke in their letter to the Spanish episcopate in glowing terms of the "heroes of the Alcazar."

The campaign of the Polish government derived its justification from, and was perhaps actually caused by, the fact that the answer of the German bishops did not contain explicitly or implicitly a recognition of the Polish western border. At the Vatican the letter of the German bishops was interpreted by most observers as having the function of preparing the Catholic population of the Federal Republic of Germany on a psychological level for the renunciation of the territories east of the Oder-Neisse line. Indeed, the multifaceted text lends itself to this interpretation, too. Insofar as this can be justified, the letter was decidedly more positive than the Polish authorities were willing to admit. But what induced the vast majority of the readers of the letter throughout the western world to believe that precisely that was the way in which it had to be interpreted? After all, there were—as we have pointed out—numerous other possibilities of interpretation. The point would seem to be that outside of the Federal Republic of Germany it has become difficult if not impossible to imagine that politicians (or leading churchmen) can think seriously of a revision of the Oder-Neisse line. Even the politicians representing the displaced Germans will hardly persist in considering such a revision a realistic possibility. Acutally, the role of the political representatives of the displaced, which was doubtless of social significance in the early days of the integration of the refugees in Western Germany, begins to appear anachronistic. But these men live politically and economically from the institutionalization of their role.

There are hardly any German politicians left who believe in the possibility of a future revision of the Oder-Neisse line. (Even cabinet members representing the viewpoint of the Christian

Democratic Union feel free to say so in private conversations.) The proposal of a barter deal with the reunification of the two German states as the price for which recognition of the Oder-Neisse line could be bought cannot be regarded as much more than a maneuver engaged in to cover the retreat. Since no neighbor of Germany is really eager to have reunification come to pass and since the Germans have meanwhile come to understand that they cannot fight "a world of enemies," one accepts for better or worse the status quo, although—as witness the Hallstein Doctrine —the Adenauer era continues to exert its political hold.

One would like very much to answer in the affirmative the question as to whether the German bishops are in a position to visualize the situation with all that is implied in it. In the world city of Rome, which has a grandiose diplomatic tradition, this is bound to be regarded as self-evident. It seems impossible to assume that a bishop should be naive enough, indeed, should be possessed of the requisite degree of political infantilism to continue under the now prevailing circumstances to believe in the possibility of a revision of the Oder-Neisse line. It is for this reason that the German reply to the letter of the Polish bishops was interpreted in Rome as intended to prepare the public on a psychological plane for a definitive renunciation. In Poland, in Czechoslovakia, and in the Soviet Union, on the other hand— that is, in countries where the Germans are respected because of their economic efficiency but where their sadism is known, too— this interpretation was not accepted as correct and instead the prevailing assumption was that the German bishops were playing politics.

I believe that the truth, as so often, lies somewhere between the two extremes. We may take it for granted that most German bishops know that the Oder-Neisse border is an established fact. They are, however, too cowardly to say so openly. Others may very well be naive enough to think that the matter is not as yet completely settled. It would then appear that the many-faceted character of the letter reflects the multiplicity of opinions represented in the German episcopate and in the German government.

The controversy between the Polish government and the Polish bishops that followed the exchange of the letters had the effect that all the Catholic groups in the Sejm dissociated themselves from the text of the letter of their bishops. That was grist for the mills of the professional anti-communists in the Federal Republic of Germany. Especially Roegele of the *Rheinischer Merkur* was gloatingly delighted. For from his point of view—he had, in fact, been most vociferous in expressing his disapproval of the policies of John XXIII whose political attitude was simply incomprehensible to him—any kind of cooperation between Catholics and communists was unthinkable. These differences proved to be advantageous to the Christian Democratic Union. The Polish bishops were represented as having intended to initiate a discussion of the Oder-Neisse border. Hansjakob Stehle was thus quite right when he criticized Roegele for stating that the letter of the Polish bishops reflected a desire on the part of its writers to "dissociate themselves from Potsdam." In a way, however, Roegele was not completely wrong either. After all, the Polish bishops had used language that might be taken to signify that they wished to express to their German colleagues their regret that the border regulation had been settled by the great powers at Potsdam.

Archbishop Kominek gave two interviews during his sojourn in Vienna, declaring unambiguously

that the Oder-Neisse border had definitive validity,
that the Potsdam agreement had been of positive significance from the Polish point of view,
that Poland did not see its function in being a bulwark against the east but in constituting a bridge, and
that the memorial of the Evangelical Church in Germany deserved to be evaluated as "highly positive."

The foregoing assertions made by the Archbishop in the interview he gave Hansjakob Stehle of the *Rheinischer Merkur* were supplemented by what he said in an interview with Dr. Kurt Skalnik, that is

That the negative reaction in Poland did not begin until part of the German press interpreted various passages in the letter of the bishops as signifying that those bishops meant to intervene in the current problems of politics and were attempting to adopt a policy of their own relative to Germany.

Both Hansjakob Stehle and Dr. Skalnik treated Archbishop Kominek with intelligent forebearance. They did not embarrass him by suggesting that he take a stand relative to the letter of the German bishops. This letter was not as much as mentioned in either one of the two interviews. Had this matter come up, Kominek would have been confronted with a delicate task, indeed.

In the article by Stehle alluded to above the author wrote that the Polish government was, as it were, jealous of the bishops. That is quite correct. But it is easy to understand that in view of Cardinal Wyszynski's interrex ambitions the government considered it extremely risky to allow him to take the initiative in matters of international politics.

The letter of invitation of the Polish bishops to the Spanish episcopate has a positive corollary in the letter of invitation addressed to the Austrian episcopate. In the latter historical facts were mentioned that were intended to underline the things Poland and Austria have in common: the decisive Polish-Lithuanian intervention in the liberation of Vienna from the Turks, the fact that the Austrian occupation of Galicia was less oppressive to the Poles than other occupations, cultural correspondences, and the like. It would have been extremely easy to draft the letter so as to annoy both the communists and the socialists, particularly the latter, if, for example, the "great Catholic Engelbert Dollfuss" had been mentioned.

The letter of invitation to the Spanish bishops was less positive from the point of view of those to whom it was addressed. It may be assumed that most of the Spanish bishops are supporters of Franco, for all of them owe their appointments, in accordance with the terms of the Concordat, to having been proposed by Franco. Nonetheless, many of the Spanish bishops do not like to be reminded of the Civil War and of their Francoist-Fascist past. The letter of invitation of the Polish bishops forced them back into a role they had ceased long since to wish to play. If Cardinal Wyszynski, as we have reason to assume, was responsible for the

Spanish invitation as well, we are obliged to conclude that he is not particularly well informed on present-day conditions in Spain.

The Polish government accused the episcopate of having accepted money from the German bishops. This assertion has its basis in a report published in the German periodical *Außenpolitik* [Foreign Affairs]. It included the following passage:

> Even if we consider that the German episcopate assumes responsibility for as high a share in the expenses of the Vatican as the American, even if we consider that the Fulda Conference of bishops pays the Polish episcopate sizeable amounts of money to enable it, as it were, through interchurch assistance to exist and that thus the exchange of letters might well be assumed to reflect definite and necessary dependences, we are still confronted here with a change of attitude that is striking.[32] (The attitude referred to is that of Cardinal Wyszynski.)

The Polish bishops did not deny having received money. As bishops in an impecunious country, they explained, they had been forced to rely on funds which the Apostolic See was able to derive from wealthier countries. The currency regulations in the People's Republic of Poland permitted the bishops, when traveling abroad, to take with them not more than the equivalent of five dollars. The Polish bishops explained that their sojourn in Rome implied for them the need of money and that they had received that money via a Vatican fund from German and American church sources. The Polish government countered with a display of accountancy showing that Cardinal Wyszynski, on the basis of seven applications, had been allowed to export a total of $6,525. This sordid but therefore by no means unimportant affair requires the comment that as a matter of principle there would be nothing objectionable in the wealthy German church's giving money to the relatively poor Polish church. If the transaction were intended simultaneously as a token of penance for German atrocities in Poland, it could—indeed—be claimed to be nothing less than praiseworthy. However, the assumption that the Germany episcopate made its gift to the Polish church only under specific conditions is—to say the least—doubtful and hardly in keeping with the facts. Such a procedure would have been tactless, especially since the Polish bishops cannot be bribed. Of course, we must not underrate the psychological effect of liberal gifts. If, let us say, the Pope needs a hundred and fifty million lire for the construction of a hospital and some prelate raises this amount for him within a short space of time, it will be but natural that this prelate should never have difficulties getting a papal audience and that he will always be listened to with interest and sympathy. To be sure, there is also the possibility—less likely and certainly less frequent—that the Pope might be aware of the unintended bribery with the result that he would restrain himself only the more rigorously.

The Melchite bishops under the leadership of Maximos IV have passed a resolution which includes the following statement: "When we hear justified complaints of the masses, we shall not hesitate to speak up, even at the risk of shocking the rich who will then cease to be our benefactors." [33] From this we may conclude that it takes a certain moral effort to say things that are unpleasant to the ears of one's benefactors. The Polish church is very poor, which—in a Christian perspective—is not necessarily a bad thing, but the bishops are accustomed to certain standards, and the parishes in the rural areas of the country are in dire need of financial assistance. For that reason sizable monetary gifts could, after all, have a certain effect and exert an influence on the attitudes and public utterances of the Polish bishops.

It is quite remarkable that the Polish episcopate never thought of inviting the Russian Orthodox bishops to take part in the Polish millennium. That was a grave omission. It should have been the concern of the Polish bishops to establish peaceful relations not only with the Germans but also with the Russians. I myself emphasized in a Polish newspaper the necessity of inviting the Orthodox bishops. The Polish press in exile likewise urged the Cardinal to undertake steps in this direction. [34]

The age-old tension between the Polish Catholics and the Russian Orthodox churches is further aggravated by the fact that Cardinal Wyszynski obviously considers the Orthodox bishops to be puppets of the regime. Still, at the Council in Rome no distinction was made between "regime bishops" and others. The Spanish bishops (by the grace of Franco) were recognized no less than the Czech and Hungarian bishops. There have always been stubborn prelates and malleable prelates. In any event, the remonstrances of various "laymen" appear to have induced the Polish episcopate in the end to invite the World Council of Churches to come to Czestochowa. Since the Russian Orthodox Church belongs to the World Council of Churches, the Russians were thus invited after all, although—to be sure—in an indirect fashion. However, this procedure was in no way commensurate with the importance of the Russian Orthodox Church from the point of view of Polish history. Similarly, an invitation to the Evangelical Church in Germany would have been no more than fair and proper. After all, the memorial issued by that church reflected greater courage in incurring the risk of unpopularity than was ever shown by the German Catholic bishops. It was only for ecumenical reasons that these latter could not dare reject outright the memorial of the EKD.

The fact that the Polish bishops failed to invite the Russian Orthodox Church proves that their aversion to the Soviet Union is not by any means exclusively a matter of ideology but derives also from reasons of nationalism. In fact, as far as the Polish-Russian conflict is concerned, Cardinal Wyszynski did his best to pour oil into the fire. When the Polish government prevented the image of Our Lady of Czestochowa from being taken on a tour throughout Poland in the course of which it would have become the center of nationwide celebrations, the Cardinal intimated that "the Holy Virgin had been incarcerated." Did he not see the difference between "incarcerating Mary" and preventing a picture of her from being taken on a tour? The Cardinal also complained that the communists persecuted the Church in a way reminiscent of the destruction of images of Mary by Russian Orthodox Cossacks in the distant past. This observation was, to say the least, tactless and certainly was not approved of in Rome, for it was clearly disruptive with respect to the efforts of reconciliation between the Russian Orthodox and Roman Catholic churches.

To be sure, the Cossacks were not exactly a well-disciplined and well-behaved fraternity, but their actions, after all, can very well be claimed to have been reactions. Considering the archaic mentality of the times, it is not particularly surprising that they did not see fit to treat the "weaker" Polish madonna with kid gloves, for it seemed quite clear that their own madonna was the "stronger" one and hence the "better" one. To hold the Orthodox of today responsible for the iconoclastic excesses of the Cossacks seems no less absurd than the attempt to reproach the Protestants of today with the atrocities of the Swedish soldiery of Gustavus Adolphus. It would not be difficult for either the Protestants or the Orthodox to come back with full equivalent arguments. In this way we could never move forward toward peace.

The arguments used by Cardinal Wyszynski prove him to be a Polish nationalist, not to say chauvinist. The supposition that a man of this frame of mind might wish to interfere in the more recent developments in the Russian-Orthodox relations with the Roman Catholic Church as well as in the Kremlin's relationship with the Vatican does not seem to be farfetched. Quite recently Wyszynski made a skillful move. As a confirmed opponent to every kind of planned parenthood he maintained that the laws covering birth control—some of which (as the sections dealing with abortion) cannot but be rejected from the standpoint of Catholic ethics—would reduce the chances of repopulating the western areas of Poland. The implication was that the Polish government was actually promoting the objectives of the West Germans. In fact, the birth rate in Poland is extremely high, and the Cardinal could at least meet the state halfway by propagating the Knaus-Ogino method of preventing conception which had the approbation of Pius XII.

So far the Vatican has been proceeding in this area with extreme caution. Its primary interest is to come to an understanding with the Soviet Union in anticipation of the possibility of evolving on that basis some form of integration with the Russian Orthodox Church. There is thus at present a shared interest on the part of the Vatican, the Kremlin, the Russian Orthodox Church, and the Polish government to oppose the special Polish nationalism represented by Wyszynski. So far the pressure exerted on the Cardinal by the Vatican has been at most moderate. A case in point was the delay in the appointments of new cardinals.

Shortly after the differences between the Cardinal and the Polish government had reached their climax, the Vatican signed a "concordat-like treaty" with the government of Yugoslavia. This was not the first treaty with a communist country but it was the most far-reaching and for that reason the most important. The earlier treaties with Hungary and Czechoslovakia were partial in nature. The negotiations leading to the Yugoslav treaty had been going on for several years. It would have been very easy to postpone signing the treaty still a little longer. As the matter was handled, the signing amounted to a demonstration of the fact—always denied and considered meaningless by conservative and reactionary Catholic circles (to which Cardinal Wyszynski certainly belongs)—that it is possible to come to an agreement with a communist state.

Cardinal Wyszynski's policies are bound to fail in the long run, but at present they are by no means unsuccessful. The Cardinal's churches are more crowded than ever in the past. Anyone who opposes the government for this or that reason—and reasons there are aplenty—goes to church, and the church thus becomes a place of reunion for the opposition. A cardinal has not only the right but, in fact, the duty to promote church attendance, but this does not imply that all measures that can serve this objective are necessarily sound. Cardinal Wyszynski's current success in Poland is not only at odds with the basic policies of peace of the Vatican (which no one has the right to doubt, just as no one has the right to doubt the peaceful intentions of Cardinal Ottaviani), they are also at odds with current trends in the history of the world. The Cardinal's activities make of him, to paraphrase Plato, a brakeshoe on the wheel of the world.

The fact that Paul VI has been treating the reactionary Catholics with kid gloves—the reactionaries are, as a Vatican diplomat once told me, "the spoiled children of the Church"—does not signify that this will always be so. Cardinal Spellman is an example. This reactionary, who always kept in his room (as an expression of a remarkably idiosyncratic variant of good taste) a wax figure of the current pope, managed to explain in his Christmas sermon in 1966 in Viet Nam with the fitting theme, "Glory to God in the Highest, and on Earth Peace Among Men," that only an American victory could assure lasting peace.

He did this no doubt with provocative intentions. A victory of Hitler would likewise have assured some kind of peace.

It seems that Spellman suffered with the inferiority complex that is characteristic of many American Catholics as a result of their having been told for many decades that they are potential traitors. In any event, his display of "two hundred per cent Americanism" (which in the long run was not necessarily in the interest of the United States) was designed to force the Vatican to fall in line with his own views. This same Spellman was rewarded in the end for all his efforts by nothing more nor less than that he had to listen to a Vatican spokesman declaring unambiguously that Paul VI—as the rest of the world has known all along—was of the opinion that only a negotiated peace could put an end to the war. This declaration was sensational. To be sure, it had happened more than once in the past that Rome did not see eye to eye with a cardinal in this or that particular matter, but in such situations the procedure adopted had always been dictated by the clan mentality which demands—in truth or untruth—that the group present a united front. For this reason the public condemnation of the views of a bishop has been a rare if not unheard-of event. Cardinal Spellman, however, had gone too far.

Cardinal Wyszynski might be well advised to bear these things in mind. For a long time the leftist Catholic lay groups in Poland and the Polish government, too, had had the desire that a specialist from the Vatican might look over the situation in Poland from close by. In compliance with such demands, the Vatican Undersecretary of State Casaroli finally did go to Poland. He declared after his visit that he had found in Poland "a wonderful life of the Church in all social strata and all age groups" and, furthermore, that the Polish authorities had in no way placed obstacles in his path throughout the duration of his fact-gathering tour.

It would seem that Casaroli's trip had the objective of restraining Cardinal Wyszynski's intransigeance and unrealistic mysticism at least to the extent that they would no longer be able to sabotage the Vatican's eastern policies. The most sensational happenings in the course of this journey were not Casaroli's meetings with individual bishops but his conversations with leftist Catholic laymen who, after all, have much better relations with the government. Casaroli had discussions not only with Stanislaw Stomma, the leader of the Znak group of representatives, but also with Jan Frankowski, the chairman of the Christian Social Society, and even the Boleslaw Piasecki, the president of Pax.

During the Vatican Council, the *Informations Catholiques Internationales* had come out in support of the Pax group. Thereupon the French ultraconservatives had reached against their leftist Catholic brothers with all the "amiability" that is characteristic of them. For this purpose the French right-wing radicals had utilized a communication of Cardinal Wyszynski addressed to the French episcopate and consisting of nothing but polemics against the Pax. The picture of Pax drawn by Cardinal Wyszynski is a masterpiece of romantic indirection. One has the impression that the cardinal willfully disregarded every kind of distinction between fact and supposition. And the outstanding fact appears to be that the members of the Pax group make use of their right to differ on occasion with their primate. In worldly matters they side with the regime.

Against this background it appears extremely significant that Casaroli received not only Frankowski but also Piasecki whom Cardinal Wyszynski had made the butt of a frontal attack. The Casaroli-Piasecki meeting marks the beginning of the Vatican's recognition of the two leftist Catholic groups in Poland against the wishes of the cardinal, the Catholic right wing in France, and also the Catholic right wing in the Federal Republic of Germany. Since the Vatican—as we have stressed on more than one occasion —is always intent on maintaining the fiction of continuity despite the underlying presence of abrupt breaks, the encounter of Agostino Casaroli with Piasecki can only be taken as discreet evidence of a new beginning. The earlier articles against Pax and the Christian-Social Society published in the *Osservatore Romano* are to be covered with the mantle of Christian brotherly love, which means, in other words, that they are to be entrusted to the tender cares of oblivion.

In trustful reliance on our awareness of the subtlety of the hierarchic opportunism in the Catholic world such delicate gestures serve the function of suggesting that the time has come for a certain re-alignment (implying, for instance, that it is no longer wrong for the press to make the Cardinal the object of a certain benevolent criticism). This would make it possible for the Catholic press in the Federal Republic of Germany, too, to adopt a new line, provided that press is endowed with at least a modicum of awareness of things to come. In any event, the Vatican has begun to apply brakes to the reactionary forces of Polish Catholicism. It is of course still possible that the right-wing extremists in the Polish episcopate will once again undertake one of those hopeless revolts which are indeed no rarity in the history of this nation. On the other hand, there is ample evidence to suggest that reason will remain in the saddle in Poland. After all, to buck the government, the Vatican, and the Kremlin all at once is an undertaking which only candidates for suicide can seriously take into consideration.

Finally a few words are in order on the most recent developments in Poland. After the six-day war between Israel and the Arab countries, a wave of anti-Semitism flared up in Poland which was but poorly concealed as "anti-Zionism."

A fact not to be overlooked is that there has been all along within the Polish Communist Party a struggle for power in which the so-called "partisans" were pushing their claims to first-line positions. What one hears about them is not very pleasant. Whether their leaders really believe what they say is hard to determine, for it is entirely possible that they are merely trying to bolster their position by utilizing the age-old syndrome of Polish chauvinism, that is, a syndrome made up of anti-Semitic, anti-German, anti-Czech, and anti-Russian elements. This trend is extremely dangerous in purely Polish terms, for the national resources are simply insufficient for any kind of war against such a "world of enemies," even though it be only an ideological or economic war.

There are certain indications that these communist partisans seek contacts with the bourgeois partisans of the former general

"Bor," who were instrumental in the Warsaw rebellion of 1944. Such a combination would entail more than a modicum of risk.

It takes a fanatic not to admit that the tension in the Near East is a complex matter involving genuine problems for anyone with attitudes of leftist orientation. Consider, for instance, the fact that a number of Polish (and also Czech) generals knew a priori—that is, purely on the basis of factual professional information—that the Arabs simply had no chance in an armed conflict with Israel. By reason of this correct diagnosis they got fired. This is a reaction typical of a petrified establishment.

On the other hand, it is not hard to understand that numerous Jews (and Jewish descendants) among the communist intellectuals sided with Israel on the basis of a purely emotional sense of solidarity with the Jews who after all had paid during Hitler's massacres the highest blood toll relative to their total numbers.

It is to be noted that in the German Democratic Republic— with the typically German skill in carrying a principle to an extreme—the official position was pro-Arab, while no Jew was removed from his post. The same, by the way, held true for Hungary. In Poland, however, the ghost of the past arose from its grave. The defeat of Marxist principles by archaic elements of the past is as sad a spectacle as the defeat of Christian principles by revenants of pre-Christian paganism.

The point in all this is that if the "partisans" do come to power, they will not find it difficult to come to an understanding with Cardinal Wyszynski. This would be an alliance of reactionary Poland with reactionary Catholicism. The very idea makes one shudder. To be sure, official Catholicism in Poland has not so far endorsed the anti-Semitic reorientation of part of the political leadership. However, individual groups have done so, and this makes us fear the worst. A consoling reflection is that what the "partisans" have revealed of their "program" is so irrational that one cannot but suspect that the possession of real power, should they achieve it, would force them to pursue a more realistic line.

In any event, the situation in Poland remains complex. There are several foci of potential danger entailing a number of irrational possibilities.

The Vatican and Czechoslovakia

The historical determinants in present-day Czechoslovakia are extremely complicated. In terms of our major preoccupation, Czechoslovakia represents, however, a sideshow and cannot lay claim to as detailed a treatment in this study as Poland.

The dynamics of the situation is basically less far-reaching. By contrast to Yugoslavia, for instance, Czechoslovakia occupies no position apart from the rest of the communist world. Politically Czechoslovakia remained for a long time clearly subordinate to the Soviet Union. It was slow in its de-Stalinist reform, though it is true that the Czechoslovak de-Stalinization, once underway, went farther than elsewhere. There is within the country an element of national tensions between the Czechs and the Slovaks, and this is clearly apparent within the Church, too, although one might have supposed that the precarious situation of Roman Catholicism in the country would unite the Czech and the Slovak clergy. Yet, during the Second Vatican Council the Slovak bishops repeatedly opposed their Czech counterparts. They did so, for instance, with respect to the question of burial by cremation.

In the Bohemian-Moravian space, history set up a stage for numerous incisive conflicts of both religious and national implications. The forced symbiosis of Czechs, Germans, and Jews resulted in a fascinating cultural atmosphere to which Prague in particular bears witness today as it has been doing throughout past centuries. The fact that even Christianity proved unable to set up in this space a model for the peaceful coexistence of various nationalities contributed to no small extent to the collapse of the Hapsburg Empire and became strikingly manifest with the expulsion of the Sudeten Germans in 1945.

Throughout the country one sees churches with spires carrying a chalice to symbolize the triumph of the Hussites over Rome. The magnificent monument of the Hussite leader John Zizka in Prague not only commemorates the early phenomenon of a "people's army" that proved virtually invincible but also the role of the Catholic priest John Huss who died for his faith at the stake in Constance. As long as the Catholic Church refuses to do penance for this crime, as long as John Huss is not rehabilitated, there will be tension between the national pride of the Czechs on the one hand and Catholicism on the other.

The demand of "the cup for the laity" has a long tradition among the Czech people, going back to the Hussites and other brotherhoods. It is the expression of a profound longing for human equality and fraternity. The priest must not have the exclusive privilege of partaking of Christ's blood. The haughty attitude of Rome which—by contrast to the Orthodox churches—denies the laity the cup has done a great deal of harm in this part of the world. As recently as 1918, Rome preferred a schism in Czechoslovakia to yielding in the question of a Czech national liturgy. In this way the Czech National Church came into being which is still the second strongest in the country. One sometimes has the impression that the Czech clergy, insofar as it represents the Church, cannot quite rid itself of a feeling of guilt toward its own nation.

In Czechoslovakia communism and socialism had a broad basis in the population. This again may have been an expression of the old longing for equality. The close ties of the Czech communists with the Soviet Union has more than one cause. This explains why Soviet models were often adopted in a spirit of slavish imitation, to the great detriment of the country's economy.

As long ago as the days of the Austro-Hungarian monarchy the Czechs were engaged in a struggle of national defense against German nationalism and German imperialism. The Sudeten Germans, particularly in the west and north of the country, flirted with the empire of Bismarck. Then, too, there was the fact that the bourgeoisie—not only during the monarchy but also in the new Czechoslovakia in the years since 1918—was predominantly composed of Germans, implying that the national tensions assumed the character of a class struggle: the Czech proletariat against the German bourgeoisie. In their opposition to German imperialism the Czech needed powerful allies, and among these Russia was naturally the most important. This accounts for the traditional feeling of friendship the Czechs have for the Russians. After the expulsion of the Germans in 1945, Czech reliance on the Soviet Union came to be tantamount to Czech dependence on the Soviet Union which represented the best guarantee against German retaliation.

When the communists came to power in 1948, they had the backing of a strong electorate. They also had the advantage of taking over the government in a highly industrialized country, a country with high educational standards, a fully developed school system, and adequate living space. It would take us too far afield to show what domestic and international causes were responsible for the decline of the living standard. We must not lose sight of the fact that our major concern is the development of the relations between state and Church. The tension which characterizes these relations are, once again, a direct outcome of the misevaluation of communism by Pope Pius XII. The early policies advocated by the domestic church authorities proved subsequently to have been right, but they were disrupted by directives issued by the Vatican and rechanneled along reactionary lines, until finally an attitude of tolerance prevailed implying the recognition of the initial position of the Czech church leaders as acceptable.

When Gottwald took over the Czech government, Archbishop Beran conducted a solemn church service with the Te Deum, with Gottwald in the congregation and Masaryk and Benes conspicuously absent. Many communists felt that Gottwald "was going too far," although Archbishop Beran and numerous members of the Catholic clergy counted communists among their acquaintances and even among their personal friends as a result of shared experiences in concentration camps.

It was only after western ambassadors had made repeated representations with the Cardinal in the name of the Vatican that Beran finally agreed to a decisive realignment. At the Vatican the idea prevailed that it would not take the Americans long to chase the communists away. (Pius XII was a man opposed to the atom bomb, but only when in addition to the Americans, the Russians had one, too.) However, the Americans did not come. The communists stayed in the saddle. And the net result was that good Catholics had been made to fight a hopeless battle and spill in it their last drop of blood. Archbishop Beran was not treated too badly, thanks to the fact that the communists, too, understand the requirements of a hierarchy. The small fry, however, laymen, parish priests, and chaplains, fared considerably worse.

The official attitude of the hierarchy met with a strong opposition within the Church under the leadership of the then Minister of Health Plojhar. Neither Beran nor Plojhar had a clear program, as little as did subsequently the so-called peace priests (whom certain western observers have at times suspected of being wolves, that is, communists, in sheep's clothing). They rather behaved in accordance with the routine pattern of the traditional monarch-devoted clergy with a strong Josephinian element of state-church predilection. Just as the official publication of the Diocese of Vienna has had from its inception an uninterrupted history of advocacy of every change of government that has occurred from 1918 to 1945, Beran, too, considered it virtually a matter of routine duty to celebrate the accession to power of the communists—for "every authority comes from God." This clerical endorsement of the powers that be is rooted in history. When subsequently the Vatican, being the highest authority, demanded resistance against the communists, there was a "conflict of obedience" involving two different authorities.

Plojhar was driven by his hatred of the Germans (understandable after his concentration-camp experiences) to side with the communists. It is likely that his ideas of what the future developments would be like were somewhat clearer than Beran's. In any event, both Plojhar and Beran must have sensed—by contrast to Pius XII—that communism did have a future. Both were politically of a leftist orientation—both having been in concentration camps—and their conviction that the communists would stay in power for a long time to come entailed the understanding that the policies of the Vatican with respect to the communists were fundamentally wrong.

There can be no doubt but that Plojhar saw more clearly than Pius XII how the political development was shaping up. If the Holy Ghost is involved in making men see things clearly, it appears to have favored Plojhar over Pius XII in its provisions of enlightenment.

It is quite possible that Beran sensed as fully as Plojhar did what the future had in store. But he allowed obedience to prevail over understanding. Obedience is a childish virtue. It crowns cowardice. Beran was rewarded for his obedience with a cardinal's hat. Plojhar, on the other hand, was excommunicated. This Roman power mechanism (which equates being Catholic with being obedient against a man's better knowledge) has nothing to do with Christianity but a great deal with the discipline of Roman cohorts and legions that were called to arms to conquer the world.

Beran sacrificed his better understanding to obedience. He sent thousands of good Catholics down a path of battle that took them to prison and untold hardship. But the conflict must have gnawed in his soul until he was called to Rome to be made a cardinal. This does not alter the fact that Rome had in truth dropped him. In this case the cardinal's hat was only a salve applied to the wound in the man's soul—the wound caused by his having sacrificed understanding to obedience.

In many respects, however, Beran derived greater wisdom from the inner conflict. When he spoke at the Vatican Council, he showed considerable understanding of the failings of the Church but no trace of that typically Catholic arrogance which claims a monopoly on truth. He pointed out that "we burnt the Catholic priest John Huss" and stated that the Church in Czechoslovakia was paying the penalty it incurred by its intolerance in former centuries. He insisted that it was not enough for the Catholic Church to demand tolerance. Tolerance, he said, was a two-way street. The stress he placed on his advocacy of freedom may well have been motivated by more than his desire to obtain freedom for the Church in his country. It may well have had the objective of assuring the Catholics within the Church a greater degree of freedom so that they might be spared the grave conflict between better understanding and obedience.

Plojhar chose to go the other way and wound up in spiritual confusion. He refused "in political matters" to be obedient to the Vatican and suffered the penalty of excommunication. To be sure, this was rescinded by a Czech bishop but hardly on strictly "canonical" grounds. As Cardinal Beran explained correctly at the Council, the Church in Czechoslovakia carried a heavy burden of guilt. But, if this is true, it is equally true that the Vatican's lust for power and papal claims to supreme authority resulted in grave wrongs being done unto the Czech church. After the Vatican's about-face decree of 1948 there was as a result a strong tendency among the Czech clergy to advocate secession from the Catholic Church. Plojhar opposed this trend. Without his influence a major portion of the Roman Catholic clergy would have defected to join the Czech National Church.

Plojhar's attitudes engendered new conflicts for him. In the clash of understanding and obedience he had opted against the latter. Yet in Catholic schools, particularly in the institutions preparing for the priesthood, it is not the prophetic spirit of resistance but the discipline of obedience that is being drilled. That is why a member of the clergy—no matter how sound his reasons may be for acting in a certain way, no matter how profoundly he may be convinced of having truth on his side—will not be able to escape an oppressive feeling of guilt whenever he resists an established authority. His clerical superego (under the principle of obedience) collides with his conscience (the principle of truth). To make matters worse, he has to realize that he is excluded from the community with which he feels at one and which he would like to serve. Indeed, it is easier to follow the path chosen by Beran than the one chosen by Plojhar. To withstand in such a situation the forces of moral corruption is extremely difficult. When a man under such conditions falls victim to corruption, the greater share of the blame must be borne by those reactionaries who drove him into the impasse.

Plojhar was caught up more and more in the fangs of the state which soon revealed its progressively Stalinist character. Since Plojhar was isolated from the hierarchy, he willy-nilly had to go along to a much greater extent than would have been necessary if the Vatican had given Beran a free hand. He drowned his inner conflicts in barrels of wine. The irony of the situation was that it was now Plojhar who represented the most important obstacle in the way of a rapprochement of the government of Czechoslovakia and the Vatican. The deal which the Vatican was willing to make with the government seems perfectly clear.

In keeping with the traditional rules of the "art of government" of the Pope, Rome could not admit that Pius XII had been wrong. For this reason Plojhar was to resign as Minister of Health, and in exchange for this his excommunication could be rescinded on "canonically" solid grounds.

This was the situation when the democratizing tendencies in the Communist Party of Czechoslovakia achieved a decisive breakthrough. The extent of the early success of that development could not have been anticipated. To be sure, after the fact one can find all sorts of explanations, such as the century-old democratic tradition of the Czechs and the like. The name of Dubcek, symbol and agent of a movement, was of a sudden world famous. The "miracle" was that a communist regime proposed to function without censorship, without special laws, that it proposed to make no claim to being above criticism, and that it intended to treat communist slogans—such as "the Party of Workers"—as realities instead of as empty phrases. Even from the communist point of view there was no longer room for either Plojhar or many of the "priests of peace" who had been collaborating with the Novotny regime. The situation was now fundamentally different. The communists granted the Catholics normal rights demanding in exchange no concessions from the Vatican.

The United Church which had been forced under Novotny to affiliate itself with the Orthodox order in a procedure familiar from the Ukraine and Rumania was able to reconstitute itself and to enter again into full possession of its houses of worship. Since the new leaders were against everything that had been introduced under Novotny, they instinctively favored the United Church and opposed the Orthodox. To do so, they required no instigation from Rome.

This fact was obviously not the sole reason driving the Soviets to the desperate act which the occupation of Czechoslovakia obviously was. It must, however, be listed among the contributory motives.

We have alluded in an earlier context to the contradiction (which in the long run and the last analysis is bound to prove crucial) of the increasing numbers of intellectuals in the Soviet Union and the attempt to keep them on a restricted diet of information. The progressivists in Prague undertook to resolve that contradiction by abolishing censorship. That they were willing to lay themselves open to the criticism they could not but foresee is proof of their courage. It also proves the honesty of their trust and the genuineness of their faith in their cause. The willingness to respond on a continuous basis to constructive criticism presupposes a high degree of elasticity of thought. What could be anticipated was that Czechoslovak communism would become involved in an unceasing process of dialogues and dialectics as the stimulus to ever-new creative solutions. The decision to adopt this new course—dispensing with the inertia engendered by censorship and the monotony resulting from the regimentation of opinion—was bold indeed.

The faith in communism which the progressivists thus displayed is as superior to the motivation of orthodox communists as the faith of the Catholics of leftist orientation is to that of the right-wing Catholics.

In the long run Moscow will not be able to resolve its currently major dilemma by anything less than an equally bold and risky step. It will have to abandon one side in favor of the other, and it cannot rid itself of its intellectuals in order to preserve its system of. censorship. To be sure, all this represents a massive challenge to the available creative energies. During the Czechoslovak "crisis," those in command in the Soviet Union proved unable to accept the challenge. Their faith in their cause was not strong enough. They did not believe in their ability to meet the intellectual challenge.

The Czechoslovak venture of the Kremlin could only serve to intensify the conflicts within the Soviet Union. The Soviet tanks rolling into Czechoslovakia were rolling against inner-Russian forces as well.

Still another Soviet problem became acutely intensified as a result of the developments in Czechoslovakia. We refer to the problem of the nationalities represented in the Soviet Union.

It would be unfair to insist that the situation in the Soviet Union relative to the problem of nationalities has not improved compared to what it was under the czars. Still, the non-Russian nationalities do not enjoy full equality with the Russians. In particular in the Ukraine, a Soviet republic bordering on Czecho-slovakia, the nationalities problem has not been given a really fair solution.

There was in Czechoslovakia a broadcasting station whose pro-grams were specifically designed for the Czechoslovak Ukrainian minority. These programs were heard in the Ukraine, and so the Ukrainians learned that Czechoslovakia was to be reorganized as a federation of Czechs and Slovaks, that the United Church had again been instituted, and many other things of similar import.

This naturally reawakened the dormant national demands, giving the Soviet Union still another reason to feel endangered in its stability. Once again, there was no readiness to look for a creative solution. All one could think of to cope with the situa-tion was repression.

The conflict between the Soviet Union and Czechoslovakia has by no means run its course. We may be certain that the ultimate victor will not be the Kremlin.

In terms of the political questions involving the Church, which represent our special interest, all this signifies that an under-standing with the Vatican might well come about on the basis here envisaged—the basis represented by the Czechoslovak model. We merely have to assume that Rome will continue to keep its imperialistic claws retracted.

It would not be bad at all if the Catholic Church could finally see its way clear to rehabilitate the Catholic priest John Huss whom the Church itself burnt at the stake.

It is difficult to avoid speculating on what might have hap-pened if the Vatican, from the very beginning, had accepted Beran's approach. There can be little doubt but that the pres-sure against the Church in Czechoslovakia would have been stronger, but this must not be exaggerated and we cannot as-sume that there would have been incisive disruptions in the Church structure. All in all, there is reason to believe that the Church would have weathered the storms of the Stalinist era better, and it seems certain that its position today would be stronger. Now the Church has to catch up and attempt to do belatedly what it failed to do when the moment called for it. In any event, the contractual agreements, abrogated or not, which

Agostino Casaroli negotiated in Prague are a possible basis for future constructive developments.

The Vatican and Hungary

Up to the time of the agrarian reform in 1945, which broke up the great estates, Hungary was essentially a feudalistically structured country. The mentality of the princes of the Church was patterned to a large extent after the social concepts of the landowning class. The Hungarian Church was still in possession of enormous holdings—in an age which (seen from a vantage point outside of Hungary) could only be defined as an age of liberal capitalism. Twenty per cent of the Hungarian land belonged to the Church. The rural population constituted a rural proletariat whose poverty could hardly be equaled elsewhere in Europe. The First World War and the upheavals marking its conclusion had done little to change the fact that Hungary danced to the tune of the Hungarian landed gentry.

Whoever goes to Hungary should not fail to visit Esztergom, the seat of the Archprimate of Hungary. The city of Esztergom itself is little more than a provincial town. Above it rises the gigantic church of the primate glorifying the princes of the Church more than it glorifies God. Christian humility was not an outstanding characteristic of the members of the hierarchy of Christ's Church. The bishops lived the life of secular princes. They resided in palaces with gorgeous suites of apartments and had at their beck and call an army of servants. They did not have to live from gifts of the faithful. They had their own estates. Proudly they kept aloof above their flocks. Who would have expected them to "sink as low" as to permit that Church rabble to support them?

Naturally, there were in Hungary, too, open-minded Christians who understood that it was not possible to play at Middle Ages in the world of the twentieth century which, after all, is a world of basic reconstruction. When they read the gospel they could not but feel ill at ease because the reality of the Church in Hungary bore so little resemblance to the life of poverty and modesty demanded by Christ. During the years between the two World Wars, individual priests were bold enough to preach that the

Church should give up its estates. However, the bishops knew how to deal with such dereliction of duty. The guilty were simply forbidden to speak. And the priests placed obedience above truth, discipline above conscience, for that is what they had been trained to do. Once again the bishops had made use of the possibility of "squelching the spirit." And the spirit had to choose, once again, a roundabout way.

After 1945 there was initially a coalition government, with the essentially Christian Small-Landowners Party as the strongest participant. This government decided to carry out the agrarian reform that had been overdue for two centuries. Cardinal Mindszenty was no advocate of this agrarian reform that would have given the Church the chance to humbly climb off its high horse of Magyar master-racism. Still, as late as 1956 Mindszenty considered the agrarian reform a grave injustice.

In Hungary, too, the peasants were hungry for land, and they hated the estates of the Church as much as they hated the estates of the magnates. It is not hard to imagine how the Hungarian peasants felt about the enormous latifundia of the Church. We need but recall how the Austrian peasants in the vicinity of the large land-owning monasteries (which are but vestiges of the Church's former feudal wealth) often hate these establishments, although in Austria the Church holdings in arable land —by contrast to the Church-owned forests—are relatively insignificant.

What would have happened if the Hungarian episcopate, between the two World Wars, had seen fit to comply with the demand for the distribution of the lands of the Church among all farmers? Even in the eyes of the most fanatic communist the Church would have appeared as a progressive power. To be sure, the Church would still have had to suffer at the hands of Stalinism. After 1956 the leaders of the Soviet Union finally understood that it was absurd to simply export the Soviet system without modification to countries of a totally different historical background. At that time there would have been a basis for fruitful cooperation with the Church. Yet, Mindszenty's stubborn perseverance in inner-Church feudalism prevented him from supporting the liberal communists. Instead, he poured oil into the fire and helped bring about the intervention of Soviet troops. The brutality with which this intervention occurred is certainly to be rejected, but this should not prevent us from understanding that the Soviets had to protect their own vital interests.

Actually, Mindszenty, who certainly never understood what communism is all about, was not—in all his stubbornness—completely uninfluenced by what was going on in the world. In an address delivered by him on November 3, 1956, he stipulated among other things: "We want to be a classless society living in a state governed by law and justice . . ." [35] This, in a way, is demagoguery, for what Mindszenty meant by "class" was obviously quite different from the Marxist meaning of the term, for he continued: ". . . in a country that is dedicated to the further development of our democratic achievements and that limits private property fairly and appropriately on the basis of the interests of the total social body . . ." [36]

We must remember under what external conditions Mindszenty delivered the address from which the foregoing quotations have been taken. Budapest was surrounded by a ring of Soviet tanks. That the communists consider the question of private property important is a point which even Mindszenty appears to have understood. For this reason he felt it wise to restrain himself somewhat in this particular matter. But a "fair and proper" restriction of private property was obviously to his mind something quite different from what it would mean to a communist. Mindszenty wished to restore private property in the old sense of the term. Like other reactionaries he does not understand the distinction of means of consumption and means of production. Yet, without this distinction it is impossible to take a meaningful stand with respect to the objectives of Marxism, for it is only the means of production, not those of consumption, that Marxism wants to see socialized.

Slighting this distinction is demagoguery, for whoever slights it wittingly can only wish to talk people into believing that socialization of factories goes hand in hand with all citizens being robbed of their beds, their refrigerators, and family cars. This line of argument implies that it is the duty of a good Christian to defend the portfolios of the industrialists. It is hardly necessary at this point to dwell at length on the fact that there have been many cases in which communist governments extended their expropriation proceedings beyond the means of production. When this happened, the procedure can only be construed as an act of revenge on the part of those who were previously suppressed.

When Cardinal Mindszenty spoke of private property he clearly had in mind the system of private ownership of the means of production, and it was this system that he wished to see restored with "fair and proper" restrictions. In the social doctrine of Catholicism, "fair and proper" is what has been, provided it is useful to the Church as an institution. All that needs to be said on this score has been said by Ernst Karl Winter and August M. Knoll. There is an apparatus of vacuous formulas by means of which it is possible to adjust the interpretation of the concepts as the occasion requires.[37]

In this connection the question arises as to what consequences the restoration of private ownership of the means of production in Hungary would have had for the Catholic Church. Compared to its feudal holdings in lands, the share which the Church had in the country's industry is not worth mentioning. We must therefore assume that the new order which Cardinal Mindszenty longed to see established would have proved to be in essence the old order, with minor improvements to be sure. It goes without saying that he saw nothing unjustified in the Church's private ownership of agricultural means of production. We may doubt whether the "fair and proper" restriction would have entailed incisive changes in the administration of the estates of the Church.

With respect to the social benefits which the Church granted its lay workers, it lagged far behind western feudal landlords and capitalists. In all Church-run establishments the employees are in practice forbidden to organize, and the "representatives of the personnel" are appointed from above. The social conditions prevailing at the Vatican are archaic. There are no unions.

Instead of calling for greater freedom within the Church—which would really have been his duty—Mindszenty advocated the reconstruction of conditions of ownership that would have meant a return to the Middle Ages. The fiasco that followed could have been foreseen. And it did follow without delay. Cardinal Mindszenty landed in the American Embassy where he performs the function of a conversation piece. He reads mass for the Americans and writes sermons for them which they do not like.

At the Vatican Mindszenty's attitude was a matter of controversy even at the time of his condemnation. Pius XII was among those who admitted that he was not quite in agreement with Mindszenty. He expressed his doubts for instance in a conversation with Friedrich Heer who was in Rome at the time. It seems that Heer had been suspected of this or that heresy and had been invited to come to Rome where he lectured at the Gregoriana. Then he was called to one of the rare night audiences of Pius XII. The Pope asked him—naturally without real interest —about his family. Heer promptly produced a snapshot which the Pope took, but instead of looking at it he began pacing up and down excitedly. In the process the snapshot was all crumpled up. Pius XII was a man of refined manners. Such men do not crumple up snapshots except in states of extraordinary inner excitement. Heer's family was completely forgotten and the Pope asked his visitor repeatedly with reference to the Mindszenty affair: "Did we do the right thing?" [38]

Breza has told us what Father Leiber, S.J., said about Cardinal Mindszenty. The things Mindszenty did were "utterly irresponsible" and "if it were not for his high office, the man would have to be shot." [39]

When Austria's Cardinal König took a surprise trip to Hungary, he was exclusively interested in seeing Cardinal Mindszenty at the American Embassy. He did not even take the time to telephone Archbishop Hamvas who is in fact, if not in name, the representative of the Hungarian Church. This did not please the Hungarians very much.

König's visit was kept a strict secret. The attempt to assure that it would remain so required the cooperation of the Austrian Ministry of the Interior (socialist at the time), which had control over visas and customs, with the Austrian Foreign Office (likewise socialist at the time), which placed a motor car at the disposal of the cardinal for the purpose of assuring that his trip would not attract the attention of the press. The plan was not entirely successful, and when König was asked later on· by a journalist what the purpose of his trip had been, he explained that he had gone to see the Primate of Hungary because he had never had a chance to make his acquaintance. It would have been wiser to simply refuse to answer the question. This could have been done firmly and still politely. After all, no one believes that the two cardinals talked exclusively about the weather or about the Second Vatican Council. There is reason to surmise that the real purpose of König's trip involved a plan to have Mindszenty taken to Rome where he could have been given any of a number of meaningless assignments.

The Hungarian government appears to hold—rightly so, no doubt—that the cardinal inside the American Embassy is less prone to cause trouble than he would be if he were in Rome. His sermons to the Americans will hardly exert an influence on American policies. From the point of view of the Vatican the present situation likewise appears to represent the best possible solution. After all, taking another reactionary to Rome is like carrying coals to Newcastle. And what else could one do with Mindszenty? He has advanced to the rank of a hero, and it is not Rome's custom to unmask false heroes.

It is unfortunate that the majority of the Hungarian bishops appears to have derived no useful lesson from the entire situation. Sometime ago I had occasion to present to a group of Hungarian bishops a lecture on Catholicism of leftist orientation. The subject struck no receptive chord in any of them. Several were shocked and settled the matter by stating: "What that man wants is a Church of beggars." [40] Any suggestion along those lines obviously strikes men accustomed to living in palaces as either impertinent or absurd. It is inconceivable to them that Jesus—here and now—would send out his apostles "without luggage" and "without funds."

Yet the news of the dialogue has reached Hungary with western Catholics and communists as messengers. I have heard Hungarian communists complain without dissimulation that they have no Catholic partners in conversation because, as they put it, "we suppressed them." To be sure there are many whose natural duties would seem to include the readiness to carry on the dialogue with the communists. The difficulty is that they lack all contact with the present.

Janos Kadar was able after 1956 to introduce step by step a more liberal regime. Hungary has a relatively high standard of living, and the Hungarians enjoy, relatively speaking, a fair amount of liberty. In matters of Church politics there has likewise been a progressive development toward more liberal attitudes, particularly since the time of the agreement with Agostino Casaroli in Budapest. In November 1966, during the opening ceremonies of the ninth Party Convention of the Hungarian Socialist Workers Party, Kadar stated in an address to the Central Committee:

Hungary has freedom of religion. The Party avoids everything that might hurt the feelings of religious men and women. Still, it goes on fighting for the dissemination of the scientific approach to reality. On the basis of our experience we welcome the dialogue which is developing in the western countries between Marxists and Christians. Its objective is the probing for modalities permitting joint action in the interest of peace. [41]

It is in keeping with the facts that Hungary strives "not to hurt the feelings of religious men and women," though this is done with a certain supercilious condescension, out of consideration, as it were, for those poor superstitious innocents who still believe in the Christ Child. To make a communist doubt the "scientific" character of his ideology is not a promising venture, although it seems quite obvious that what is fascinating in Marxism are its ethical and eschatological elements and not its scientific trappings. The glorious vision of the future that is characteristic of Marxism is at best a working hypothesis. But for working hypotheses men are not generally ready to sacrifice their lives. The idea that the "scientific ideology" of Marxism demands of its advocates that they "fight" for it instead of simply "working" for it, is communist party jargon.

Kadar welcomes the dialogue. He thus accepts the gift of the Second Vatican Council to the world. It pays most certainly to talk to Hungarian communists. There is, despite Mindszenty, hope for the future—in Hungary and for Hungary.

The Vatican and Yugoslavia

The situation in Yugoslavia has been complex ever since the country after 1918 was first set up in its present form, embodying Serbia, Montenegro, and parts of the Hapsburg monarchy. There is a great deal of friction between Croats and Serbs who use different scripts (although their language is practically the same) and who profess different forms of the Christian creed. There is tension, too, between Christians and Mohammedans, but these play at most a subordinate role relative to the position of the Catholic Church.

The Croats are traditionally pro-German and Roman Catholic. They hate both the Italians and the Orthodox Serbs. The most vicious and basest excess of Croat nationalism was the Ustachi movement for which mass murder was a matter of course. It sided with the German forces of occupation. It called itself Catholic.

The mentality of the Croats at the time is illustrated by the way in which a clergyman during religious instruction elucidated the fifth commandment: "Of course one must not kill, but it happened once during the First World War that in summertime a soldier had to take back an Italian prisoner. Because it was so hot and because it took so long to walk, he threw the Italian into a gorge. Well, the prisoner was an enemy. So it wasn't really so bad."

It would be absurd to claim that that was the way the Croat clergy thought. The point is merely that such a story could get going. There is something here to account for the cruelty of the Ustachi.

The relationship of the Ustachi to the Church during the last war and shortly thereafter was extremely problematic. The bands of the Ustachi included in some instances clergymen. Orthodox victims were given the alternative: become Catholic or die. Many chose death and thus became martyrs of their faith.

The *Führer* of the Ustachi was Ante Pavelich, an infamous criminal of the format of an Eichmann. The Ustachi massacres of Jews, Serbs, and Orthodox Croats were surpassed, as Seton-Watson [42] put it, only by Hitler's mechanized murders in Poland. The former German general Rendulic,[43] who was of Croat descent and claimed profoundly that the Croats are Slavicized Goths, has left us the record of a conversation he had with Pavelich. Rendulic mentioned that he had heard that the Ustachi had killed 500,000 people. Pavelich called this calumny and slander: "It was only 300,000." If Pavelich had had at his disposal Hitler's armed power (and Hitler's inexhaustible reservoir of potential victims), he would not have to play second fiddle in the concert of monsters of our century.

On the occasion of Pavelich's visit to Rome, Pope Pius XII gave a great reception. This confirmed Catholics and non-Catholics in their belief in a link of Catholicism to the Ustachi.

Little is known about the personal views of the then cardinal —Aloysius Cardinal Stepinac—on the Ustachi and their atrocities. Neither the Catholic nor the communist information on this score can be taken at face value. There can be no doubt but that a relationship did exist between Stepinac and Pavelich, but this should not be taken as an excuse for jumping to conclusions. It is quite possible that Stepinac was an enemy of the Ustachi but did not wish to lose contact with the man who had come to be head of state, for this—his reasoning may have been—would enable him to exert at least a moderating influence. To be sure, Stepinac could equally well have joined the partisans, as many Catholics were doing in Poland. It is also possible that he was thinking of breaking off his relations with Pavelich but refrained from doing so when the Pope honored Pavelich by a solemn reception. This would make Stepinac another victim of the policies of Pius XII, just as numerous Catholics of the Center Party in Germany had been sold down the river by the then Nuncio Pacelli. Finally, we cannot completely reject the possibility that Stepinac in fact had certain sympathies with the brutally domineering personality of Pavelich, implying that the contact with such a man did not really displease him. After all the Church also knows how to be domineering and reveals not infrequently a certain kinship with the fascist polar principles of command and submission.

Wherever the truth may lie, the Serbs and the Orthodox Croats (whose priests had sided with the partisans) could have no friendly feelings toward the Catholic Church. This accounts for the fact that for a while Tito's partisans in Croatia killed every priest they could get hold of. In Slovenia this was different. The Franciscans had been on the side of the partisans and continued subsequently to maintain the best possible relations with the communists.

The legal proceedings that after the war were instituted against Stepinac did not wind up in a death sentence (as they did in the case of the Slovak priest Tiso). Stepinac was sentenced to hard labor, and this was commuted to house arrest because he—like Mindszenty and Beran—had remained "steadfast" and had refused to leave the country.

Ever since the relations between the Vatican and Yugoslavia took a turn for the better, there have been those who believe that this was the fruit of the seed sown by the steadfastness of Stepinac. Nothing could be farther from the truth. The credit belongs much rather to those priests who embraced the righteous cause of the partisans. One of these was Seper, the cardinal of Zagreb. There have been many ways in which Seper tried to make up for the mistakes of the past. In doing so he provided an example of true Christianity.

Seper's attitude of profound understanding embraces also his endeavor to come to a reconciliation with the Orthodox. There is on record an account of how during the war an Orthodox church was attacked during Sunday mass by members of the Ustachi. The great majority of the local population was taking part in that service. All the faithful—men, women, and children—were brutally murdered, and the church was set on fire. Later on, the Orthodox received money from the United States for the reconstruction of their Church. Archbishop Seper induced the Catholic peasants in nearby areas to come with their teams of horses to transport the building materials for the reconstruction of the church. It is this attitude that made possible the "concordat-like treaty" between the Vatican and Belgrade. It is an attitude breathing the spirit of Pope John.

The progressive liberalization in Yugoslavia entailed a gradual re-entry of the Church into the life of the country. Today there are in Zagreb more young theologians than ever before. The Church in Croatia has meticulously refrained from appealing in any way to the baser nationalistic instincts of the faithful. On the contrary, it supports the state in its endeavors to attenuate nationalistic tensions.

Both Cardinal Seper and other bishops of the Yugoslav hierarchy—such as, for instance, Bishop Franic of Split—proved during the Second Vatican Council that they were capable of progressive leadership. This was apparent, for instance, with respect to the Jewish question and the question of poverty.

The Yugoslav "league of communists" has rescinded for its members the ruling that they must not belong to a religious organization. To be sure, this does not imply that the Communist Party likes to have its members lead the lives of active Christians or of adherents to some other faith, but it does mark a beginning.

Yugoslavia is the first communist state with which the Vatican, after the earlier break of diplomatic relations, again exchanged ambassadors. Casaroli concluded in Belgrade a treaty in this sense. There is much to suggest that the cooperation of state and Church in Yugoslavia will continue to evolve along positive lines. The very fact that Tito allowed the negotiations leading to the treaty to continue for several years appears to suggest that he intends to live up to the terms of the treaty.

The Vatican and the German Democratic Republic

As we recall the origin of the German Democratic Republic, its subsequent development, and its current status in terms of international politics, we readily understand the tensions that exist between the German Democratic Republic and the Federal Republic of Germany as well as the difficulties which the German Democratic Republic has in coping with the problems of its relations with other countries. The partition of Germany, regarded after the Second World War by the Allies—in particular by Roosevelt and Stalin—as a guarantee for the future peace in central Europe, has resulted for the two German states in fundamentally different developments, entailing the genesis of new fields of tension. The Soviets—who, after all, had borne the main burden of the war against Germany and whose losses in human lives and also in means of production had been enormous—demanded commensurate reparations. In the territories occupied by them they dismantled most of the industrial installations. To be sure, the major German industrial facilities—those in the territory of the Ruhr—were beyond their reach. That the Soviets felt no particularly warm friendship for the Germans is not very surprising.

The dismantling of installations of production in Eastern Germany and the reparations exacted from the country by the Soviet Union gave the German Democratic Republic—compared to the Federal Republic of Germany—markedly less favorable starting conditions, implying between these two states an economic gradient resulting in mass defections to Western Germany. After the economic resurgence of the Federal Republic the escape to the west was promoted by systematic efforts of publicity. These efforts, however, were not exclusively motivated by economic reasons. There was also the hope that it might result in a political undermining of the German Democratic Republic and its eventual collapse.

Western Germany disregarded the right of the Soviet peoples —of Poland, of Czechoslovakia, and its other neighbors, not excluding Austria and Switzerland—to guaranteed safety from a renewed German aggression. The existence of the German Democratic Republic provides that safety. The East Germans, insofar as they support the state, acknowledge Germany's responsibility for the Second World War (and also for the First), while the West Germans appear to believe that they won the war. In this belief they are backed by the western powers which provide the Federal Republic of Germany with substantial help. The economy of the Federal Republic of Germany, finally, achieved its comeback at least in part thanks to the availability of highly qualified manpower defected from the German Democratic Republic.

The schools in the German Democratic Republic—seen as institutions of social education and training—are thoroughly organized and display many features from which those interested can learn a great deal. However, investments in education have a way of yielding returns only on a long-term basis. In any event, the specialists who had received their training in the German Democratic Republic and who then left for West Germany represent an East German subsidy to western industry. To a lesser yet by no means negligible extent, West German industry is also subsidized in this indirect fashion by the Austrian state. The amounts involved are doubtless known to the Austrian Ministry of Education, but they are kept secret for the sake of maintaining good relations with the Federal Republic of Germany. The refugees from the German Democratic Republic represent a major debit item in that country's ledger sheets, for those who left were primarily specialists and not unskilled labor. In many instances, the men left their wives and children behind, causing a rise in the share of women in the total population. Two million refugees from the German Democratic Republic have swelled the working potential of West German industry.

The German Democratic Republic recognized the Oder-Neisse line, the Potsdam treaties, and the German war guilt and renounced categorically the possession of atomic weapons, quite in contrast to the Federal Republic of Germany which shows no inclinations in this direction. In the Federal Republic German nationalism has grown strong again. "Professional Sudeten Germans" have been making their demands of restitution, and the fiction of the borders of 1937 has been maintained. (There are only historical maps of Germany.) All this served to make clear to Germany's neighbors what importance attaches from their various points of view to the existence of the German Democratic Republic. The eastern countries say so openly, the western countries only "in private."

The East Germans, who are quite aware of the function they perform, feel rightly that they are given an unfair deal and that they are not sufficiently recognized. They bore and still bear the burden of Germany's war guilt, while the West Germans play the part of innocent gentlemen. The vicious circle in which the German Democratic Republic found itself caught up could be broken only by putting an end to the permanent economic blood transfusion. For this reason the Berlin Wall was erected.

The need for it has been recognized even by certain prominent Americans.

The Berlin Wall marked a turning point in the economic development of the German Democratic Republic. It is true, the agrarian reform precipitated once again a grave agricultural crisis, but all this is now a matter of the past. In the German Democratic Republic even the kolkhozes (called there "agricultural production cooperatives") function successfully. Today the German Democratic Republic, too, has its contingent of foreign workers, needed—in part—as a result of the manpower bloodletting represented by the escape of able-bodied workers to the west.

For a long time the German Democratic Republic felt politically insecure because few states had recognized it. Even the Soviet Union did not seem to be entirely reliable, at least not while Khrushchev was in power, negotiating with the West German ambassador Kroll in Moscow. Meanwhile a treaty has been concluded which does give the German Democratic Republic security.

An appraisal of conditions in the German Democratic Republic must take into consideration the frame of mind of the population and the caliber of the functionaries. The country can look back on an impressive tradition. Fifteen years of the Weimar Republic were followed by the Third Reich which gave way virtually without transition to the communist regime. The noncommunist parties enjoy freedom of movement only within clearly defined limits. One may feel that it would be in the interest of the communists if they were to build the values of liberalism into their system, but they are not well prepared for such a venture. They have retained the traditional Prussian-military reliance on imperatives and hence also traces of the old Prussian feudalism with its doctrinaire propensities. These elements are quite apparent on an ideological level. East German communism is unpleasantly prone to be exaggeratedly categorical in its phraseology. Italian-style liberal communism is unheard of in the German Democratic Republic.

Some sectors of the country's cultural life have been sorely neglected in the official policies. I once had occasion to see in Dresden a comprehensive exhibition of the products of the officially promoted art forms. It was a depressing experience. This low level cannot be underbid anywhere except perhaps in the Soviet Union: Girls leaning against tractors and peering into the rising socialist sun . . . It seems that communism has little more by way of symbols than the rising sun and the red star. There is in the German Democratic Republic, however, a new architecture which does command respect. Conditions are similar in the sciences which are likewise given but little freedom. The country's economy tolerates a private sector which is essentially petty-bourgeois in character.

In matters of Church politics the German Democratic Republic is amazingly liberal. No clergyman has ever been locked up. In East Berlin I once heard a sermon against the atheistic pressure in the state-run factories. Under Hitler the equivalent boldness would have landed the clergyman in a concentration camp. In any event, it is a fact that in the schools and plants and offices pressure is exerted to promote the "scientific" ideology, and it is also a fact that it takes courage not to give in to such pressure.

On the other hand, no one can claim that the Christian churches did much to impress the state with their willingness to cooperate. If they were ready to make concessions, it would no doubt be possible for them to obtain in exchange considerable benefits. This is not mere speculation. The point can be illustrated by the positive examples of the evangelical bishop Mitzenheim. He was ready to support the German Democratic Republic in its vital political endeavors and was thus able to accomplish a great many things in the interest of his church. One should not overlook that Mitzenheim's work represented a great service also to Germany's neighbors. The Catholic bishops in East Germany on the whole follow instructions issued in the Federal Republic. They make no concessions to the state. In fact they sabotage the efforts of those Catholics who wish to work for a bearable relationship to the state. Insofar as these are members of the clergy they can expect punitive transfers to particularly undesirable parishes.

The state has done a great deal to help rebuild war-damaged churches. Yet, the bishops do not consider it worth their while to even inform the competent government agencies of the appointment of a new bishop. They might at least show their faces on occasions where their presence as exponents of the Christian spirit of atonement would be meaningful, such as for instance at memorial celebrations for the concentration-camp victims. By the way, it would not hurt the West German bishops either to have a look at Buchenwald. After all, even Cardinal König visited Oswiecim during his stay in Poland.

Unfortunately one cannot escape the impression that the German Catholic bishops are in many respects less ready than the German communists to manifest a spirit of repentance. In West Germany it is now generally admitted—and that is at least something—that the massacres of Jews are to be condemned but while it is true that the losses suffered by the Jews have been enormous, this does not imply that the crimes against other ethnic and religious groups can be slighted. In the Federal Republic of Germany, the killing of Russians, Poles, Czechs, Yugoslavs, gypsies, and others seems to be regarded as at worst a gentlemen's faux pas. The German Democratic Republic does not share this opinion. All war-time murders are being punished there. The German episcopate might well learn a lesson from the East Germans.

The German Democratic Republic has a Secretary of State for Church Questions. The present incumbent of this office, Hans Seigewasser, stands sky-high above his colleagues in the other people's democracies. Until quite recently his administrative department was considered both unimportant and uninteresting, and it was not on the whole the best men that were put in charge of it. Seigewasser, however, is a man with whom it might be worthwhile to take up contact. Ulbricht, too, will not necessarily be adamant in questions concerning the Church. His contacts with the evangelical bishop Mitzenheim bear this out. The whole situation would be greatly simplified if the German Democratic Republic were allowed to emerge from its state of isolation, that is to say, if it were recognized by the other countries.

Vatican politics is strangely averse to getting involved in the problems of the German Democratic Republic, although this is a field in which a modicum of skill might go a long way. The first step would have to be the recognition of the Oder-Neisse border, followed by the recognition of the German Democratic Republic. If this seems too risky in view of West German sensitivities, it would still be possible to skirt the Hallstein Doctrine and establish a sort of "commercial mission" with consular functions or possibly a fully qualified agency for Vatican-sponsored publications. There is no shortage of possibilities. Then, too, the antediluvian diocesan subdivisions could be revised, with the East German portions placed under bona fide bishops instead of simply under suffragans.

In all such things the Vatican will naturally have to deal with a German pressure group whose significance must not be underrated. However, it is quite possible that there are numerous politicians in the Federal Republic who would personally welcome a more realistic appraisal of the German Democratic Republic. Their hands are tied, however, in view of the official political line of the West German government. If they could refer to the Vatican as a precedent, it would be simpler for them to chart a new course.

Thus we are bound to conclude that the German Democratic Republic represents an area of unexploited possibilities for the Vatican. Sooner or later these possibilities will have to be made use of in the interest of a peaceful development. The most urgent need consists in helping the people of the German Democratic Republic to achieve emancipation from their current unnatural situation. Since a reunification of Germany collides with the demand for security on the part of the remaining countries of Europe and is hence an impossible goal for a long time to come, there is nothing left one can do except to adjust to the facts as they are. The Vatican could very well be of help in preparing for the recognition of the German Democratic Republic through the modality of various semiofficial contacts.

We should not allow our hopes on this score to be thwarted by the elements of doctrinaire venom in the attitude of both the press and the leadership of the German Democratic Republic toward Czechoslovakia. That the Germans are apple polishers and love to play at being model students in order to be able to look down upon others whose communism is not as simon-pure as their own is just a manifestation of the German or rather Prussian tradition of *Kadavergehorsam*.

On the other hand, one must not overlook that a democratization of Czechoslovakia and a possible military aggression based in that country would, for strategic reasons, threaten the German Democratic Republic more grievously than any other people's republic. These facts make the hysterical intensity of the reaction of the German Democratic Republic to the events in Czechoslovakia at least halfway understandable. In addition, the leadership of the German Democratic Republic is extremely suspicious of the new course in the eastern policies of the Federal Republic of Germany. Indeed, this new course is, to say the least, ambiguous. It purports, on the one hand, to serve the aim of establishing better relations with the eastern countries but, on the other hand, the German Democratic Republic is not to be recognized. There are two ways of interpreting this ambiguity.

We may be optimists and argue that the politicians in the Federal Republic of Germany have decided to start swallowing the bitter pills of reality, beginning with the less bitter ones that are represented by the establishment of diplomatic relations with the non-German eastern countries, in order to proceed subsequently, once the population has become accustomed to the medication, with the bitterest pill of all, that is, the recognition of the German Democratic Republic.

We can be pessimists and impute to the politicians in the Federal Republic of Germany the desire to gradually win over the countries of the eastern bloc, with the exception of the German Democratic Republic, by a systematic program for the development of economic ties, with the net result being a complete isolation of the German Democratic Republic whose incorporation in the Federal Republic could then no longer be opposed by anyone.

In Czechoslovakia there was the greater trust in the intentions of the Federal Republic of Germany and of its western allies. In the German Democratic Republic there was the greater distrust. This should not be too surprising.

As a matter of fact, this is a situation which does not lend itself to an either-or interpretation. What we said as optimists fits some West German politicians; what we said as pessimists fits others. There is consensus as to the first leg of the journey, the establishment of better relations with the eastern countries with the exception of the German Democratic Republic. In the countries of the east the view is frequently advanced that American and other politicians and political scientists advise the West Germans to pursue the Machiavellian objective we ascribe to them in a mood of pessimism. But in pursuing this line of argument we need to be cautious and circumspect. There can be little doubt but that many of those politicians and political scientists have no faith whatsoever in the second phase of their plan. They believe, however, that once the West Germans have been induced to establish friendly relations with the non-German eastern states, it will be easier to induce them to recognize the German Democratic Republic, too. A wicked ultimate goal is held up, as it were, for the purpose of getting things started along the first stage of a good road. It is quite likely that such a plan would work, for whatever can be said about the Germans, they are not particularly subtle. Then, too, it is a mistake to underrate a man like F. J. Strauss. It must be understood that Strauss combines uncanny short-term cleverness with an equally uncanny ability to perpetrate long-term errors.

What, now, does all this amount to from the point of view of Vatican politics? The Vatican is incomparably more realistic with regard to the problem of the German Democratic Republic than the politicians of West Germany (provided the views of these politicians are indeed fully reflected in the official releases emanating from Bonn). The Vatican is moving—albeit slowly and with considerable hesitation—toward an ultimate recognition of the German Democratic Republic.

Casaroli's trips to Poland were a first step. He visited, among other places, the city of Stettin which belongs to the Diocese of Berlin or, to be technically precise, to the "Free Prelature of Schneidemühl." Whatever its name, the diocese or prelature lies within the territory of the German Democratic Republic. The confused complexity of this Church situation does little to improve the relations of the Church to the government of the German Democratic Republic. Since the government of the Federal Republic of Germany cannot be expected to recognize the Oder-Neisse border in the foreseeable future, it is incumbent upon the Vatican to think and act in a spirit of progressive farsightedness. The Vatican has begun to inform the German bishops of its views. Such a procedure cannot fail to exert a favorable influence on the stability of the peace in Central Europe. It certainly will not fail to exert an influence on the religious policies of the German Democratic Republic. We may attach some importance to the fact that Paul VI elevated Archbishop Bengsch to the rank of cardinal.

The Vatican and the Other People's Democracies of Europe

Apart from the countries discussed in the foregoing chapters, there are in Europe the three people's democracies of Rumania, Bulgaria, and Albania. I regret to say that what I know about these countries is not based on personal observation. In any event, the three are of only secondary significance in terms of the politics of the Vatican, and our discussion of them can be brief.

Rumania is probably the most important. It has been following —insofar as that is compatible with the fact that it is a communist country—a fairly idiosyncratic course. However, its disagreements with Moscow do not signify that its policies in religious matters must be particularly liberal. Rumania wants a revision of its borders with the Soviet Union. It would like to get Bessarabia back. Since Rumania did not take a stand against China but tried to follow a middle-of-the-road course between Moscow and Peking, the climate was favorable for an economic and political rapprochement with the Federal Republic of Germany.

The communist "upper crust" in Rumania is not particularly strong and feels hence obliged to extend and strengthen its grass-roots support by means of nationalistic slogans. The Rumanian economy is slowly moving ahead, but it will take a long time before the broad masses begin to reap the fruit of the current investments.

Several Christian creeds are represented in Rumania. The most firmly rooted is the Orthodox Church. The Uniat Church was reintegrated in about the same way as it was in the Ukraine. The Orthodox Church has excellent relations with the government. It appears that its leadership has very ambitious objectives which coincide—be it by chance or be it by design—with those of the Rumanian communists. The Russian Orthodox Church is pro-Roman in its attitudes, while the Rumanian Orthodox Church is militantly anti-Roman. It considers itself a bulwark of orthodoxy against Roman papism and continues in this respect a very old tradition. It takes a dim view of the "revisionist" Russians. There is, it is true, some evidence to suggest that the situation is undergoing a change, for the Rumanian Orthodox Church is preparing a great reception for Cardinal König. This may indicate that the state does not wish to become isolated in terms of Church politics.

While it is true that the Rumanian government suppresses the Roman Catholic Church more rigorously than the other churches, it is also true that the hold of Catholicism on the population is much weaker. The only Roman Catholic bishop of the country had his seat in Cluj (formerly known as Klausenburg). He was of Hungarian descent and had neither sympathies nor understanding for communism. There followed an incident involving the administration of the sacrament of confirmation by which he felt angered. He complained of lack of religious freedom and withdrew into his palace where he has been ever since considering himself a political prisoner. He did not attend the Second Vatican Council although the government placed at his disposal a luxury car and a special airplane. In Rome the irregularity resulting from his absence was quickly corrected. A Rumanian professor who had been asked to come to Rome as an academic expert was consecrated bishop. Now Rumania has two Roman Catholic bishops, one who is a prisoner and one who is free.

Little need and can be said about Catholicism in Bulgaria. John XXIII (before he became Pope) spent some time there as Papal Legate. Bulgaria follows in all matters the Moscow line and can be expected to do so in matters involving the Church as well. Furthermore, the Bulgarian Orthodox Church is closely linked to the life of the nation and is hence better qualified to promote Christianity in that country than the Roman Catholic Church. In Albania, the Chinese satellite in Europe, there is a Catholic Church, but apart from the fact of its existence little is known about it. No representative of it was allowed to attend the Second Vatican Council. This signifies that the Church is at best allowed to vegetate. Its future will depend on the outcome of the Chinese struggle for power.

It is certain that the Vatican will endeavor to make peace first of all with the countries of the Soviet Russian bloc. It may attempt to bring pressure to bear on those countries by pointing out what happened in Albania. This kind of "higher diplomacy" is not at all beneath the Vatican diplomats, and they know full well that the Albanian mess is something they will not have to clean up.

The Vatican and the Future of the Eastern Bloc

In the countries of the eastern bloc, the mythological and religious elements which constitute the dynamic reserves of Marxism are regarded as "scientific." The claim is that all problems can ultimately be resolved through science. This is wrong. Scientific procedures can serve to verify the tenability or to prove the inadequacy of a particular theory. The Marxist vision of the future cannot be verified nor demonstrated to be inadequate. Marxism is essentially a matter of faith.

It appears that the Yugoslavs are the most courageous Marxists. At a meeting I once had the occasion to hear a Marxist professor from Zagreb explain that there are mythological elements in Marxism and that these elements represent the dynamic content of Marxism as well as the aspect of it that is fascinating to the masses: the vision of a society of the future and the transition to it.[44]

The striving for justice as a characteristic of Marxism has likewise nothing to do with science. Communists have died and sacrificed themselves for a juster and more humane order of society. None has died and sacrificed himself for a "working hypothesis." Such martyrdom presupposes a strong faith. This faith, this belief in a just order, in a society built on ethical foundations, can be (or better: could be) integrated with the Christian faith.

It is scandalous that Christianity of the Roman Catholic persuasion has never seriously attempted to change the structure of society in a way permitting a better and more basic implementation of Christian ideals. Group ownership of the means of production is preferable to private ownership in terms of the ethics of Christianity, too. Remuneration for work done comes as a matter of course, but the great differences in the levels of remuneration that are customary in the capitalist system cannot be justified in Christian terms.

The principle of a moral commitment to society is essentially akin to Christian ethics. It will be easy to draw up a list of many additional characteristics of Marxism that are entirely compatible with Christianity.

A popular claim in the eastern countries is that the propaganda for freedom carried on in the west is nothing more than a demand of capitalist interests. This is untrue. But it is also untrue that Roman Catholicism is the ultimate fortress of freedom. In this respect it hardly behooves Roman Catholicism to cast the first stone at communism. While a system of free economy is of necessity ethically inferior to socialism (although in the economic realm, too, greater elbow room for a free development needs to be granted than most communist countries exemplify), in cultural matters anything less than complete freedom of the spirit is inferior in an absolute sense. This applies to religion, science, philosophy, art. Freedom of the spirit must never be regarded as a concession to the immature who need it because in them the wine of youth has not completed its process of fermentation. On the contrary, freedom of the spirit is necessary for the sake of the values that are to find expression in realms where the spirit rules supreme.

Both communism and Catholicism will have to learn that freedom of the spirit is a vital requirement of the propulsive powers of history, that without it the human mind cannot be creative, and that it is one of the sacred basic rights of man. A delight in the multiplicity of spiritual approaches, in the viewpoints of others, in the differentiation of opinions is essential to freedom. Both communism and Catholicism often claim that they advocate "full freedom for something" (meaning for the pursuit of their specific ideals) and do so because they do not wish to grant "full freedom from something" (for that something might often be a duty they wish to impose). However important it may be to achieve "awareness of necessity," such awareness can be achieved only when there is freedom of discussion and freedom of opinion. It is impossible to assume that some central committee has an a priori monopoly on such an awareness of necessity. That would be just as absurd as it is to assume that every word ever spoken by Pius XII was spoken by the Holy Ghost. It took John XXIII to state bluntly: "I am not infallible. The Pope is infallible only when he speaks ex cathedra. I shall never speak ex cathedra." Criticism of the hierarchy and particularly of those forming the summit of the hierarchy must not only be permitted, it must be regarded as a productive mechanism of correction to which all measures of the hierarchy are subject. As long as it is not possible to freely criticize the Pope in the press of the Church, as long as such a criticism is not in fact wanted, so long freedom cannot be said to prevail within the Church. The same applies to the systems of communism.

It is true, freedom has made inroads into the systems of the Catholic Church and of communism, but in both systems the leaders still regard freedom as an unwelcome intruder. It would be better, in their eyes, if there were no freedom; it impresses them as an imposition; they count it as a concession; it is—in their eyes—destructive. The hostility to religion that has been characteristic of communism should serve to exemplify for the Church the value of freedom. The formal kinship of communism and the Church is so strong that the two can meet only on a liberal basis. The technical advances of our era make the individual evermore conscious of the fact that mankind is one and that men must come to a mutual understanding. The more clearly this necessity is understood, the easier it will be to achieve understanding. It is bound to come. To be sure, it will not be entirely what is foreseen in the one camp nor will it be a complete fulfillment of the expectations in the other. Both parties will have to relinquish their proud claim to being in sole possession of the absolute truth. Both will have to descend to the level of realities and abandon their self-righteousness.

The antidemocratic antics in both centers—the Vatican and the Kremlin—are but a short-legged argument against the claim that democracy will ultimately be victorious in both systems. We allude here, among other things, to the encyclical *Humanae vitae* of Paul VI, which we have previously had occasion to mention. Its real, though unavowed subject was not birth control but the authority of the Pope.[45] His real concern was to demonstrate the continuity of the teaching of the Church by retaining the absurd distinction made by Pius XII between "natural" and "unnatural" means of preventing conception. He obviously felt compelled to cling to this distinction for otherwise too many people might notice that the teachings of the Church are not immutable. In other words, Paul VI tries to restore the inflated claim to infallibility of Pius XII after the interlude represented by John XXIII. The attempt could not but backfire. By renouncing all the authoritarian trappings, John XXIII had gained authority even beyond the limits of the Catholic world. By inflating his claim to authority, Paul VI—a second Pius XII slightly delayed by John XXIII—lost much of it even within the Catholic world.

Quite similarly the Kremlin lost its authority in world communism by attempting to restore it in Czechoslovakia by means of tanks. In this way both sides undermined their authority by exaggerating it. Against their will they thus dramatize and accelerate the process of democratization. Through ill-advised acts of authority a dialectic contribution is made to the process of liberalization and democratization.

In both seemingly monolithic systems, freedom and pluralism are progressing. The two blocs move closer to one another. It is quite likely that they will meet sooner than most of us are ready to believe. The time will come when a Christian and liberal communism will exist side by side with atheistic communism, and Christian communism will live longer. In the more immediate future both sides will continue to engage in a chess game of strategy and sophistry. But they will also strive to understand one another. There are, thank God, men of ethical commitment on both sides. The clever diplomats live on them. They are the most valuable chessmen the diplomats have. In the end, they will cease to be chessmen.

Regarding the Impossibility of an Ideological Coexistence

One of the stupidest inventions of our time (which is certainly not poor in stupid inventions) is the slogan of the "impossibility of an ideological coexistence." If the phrase is to signify that two ideologies cannot exist side by side, it is patent nonsense for the world is full of ideologies which do exist side by side. If on the other hand the implication is intended to be that the truth of one ideology implies that the other is wrong, then we find ourselves in the presence of so extreme a simplification that even the most naive must hesitate to parrot it.

After all, Christianity and communism do not rest each on a single assertion. A single assertion might possibly be proved to be right or wrong. The two represent much rather extremely diversified complexes in which the inner links are by no means at all times a matter of logic or ontological necessity. Psychologically, too, there is no inescapable association of, let us say, the thesis that God created the world with the principle of private ownership of the means of production or of the thesis of the infinity of the world with the demand that imperialism must be opposed. In other words, it is quite possible for one aspect of communism to be true while another is false, and the same thing holds obviously true for Christianity as well. The notions that a historically evolved aggregate of ideas may be wrong in its totality is obvious nonsense. In the realms of faith there are necessarily statements which it is not possible to prove. There will always be men who believe in God and others who do not.

It is easy to find numerous examples of men of different ideologies living side by side not only without killing one another (coexistence) but as good friends who hold one another in high esteem and prove mutually stimulating. To be sure, they will keep trying to convince one another of the correctness of their theses, but they can go on living in fellowship without hatred until they die and never succeed in changing one another's views. Indeed, there are married couples who manage to maintain this sort of tolerance, and married life under such conditions is quite often the very opposite of an ordeal. The shared basis is tolerance, respect on the part of each for the inner freedom of the other, and the recognition of common ethical "rules of the game."

The slogan of the "impossibility of an ideological coexistence" was obviously invented in the Soviet Union. Now this nonsense is being parroted by innumerable people, including many who claim to be Christians. One cannot but wonder what motive underlies that formulation. It is not difficult to find. The thesis of the "impossibility of an ideological coexistence" justifies the fight for the scientific ideology in the home country, with the justification of administrative measures against the advocates of an "unscientific ideology," while coexistence on an international plane merrily goes on being a simple fact of life.

It will have to be recognized both in the communist world and in the Church that this kind of dual standard is not tenable in the long run. Cooperation with a Christian church on the international level is incompatible with the domestic suppression of the Christian faith. No state today can manipulate its citizens as it pleases. There is a solidarity above and beyond national borders. Just as the Soviet Union cannot be disinterested in matters involving the fate of communists in other countries, so a Christian cannot be indifferent regarding the fate of his fellow believers in the Soviet Union.

The impossibility of an ideological coexistence is a favorite theme of those whose pastime is the witch hunt against "obliterators of categories and borders." A typical example is Werenfried van Straaten who believes that neoliberalism, that is, the (social) market economy à la Erhard represents the incarnation of Christian charity, because the Catholic social dogma cannot be extended beyond the level of an enlightened capitalism. But there are also dogmatic communists who imagine that they have a completely closed system from the structure of which no stone and no pebble may be removed.

But the pluralistic trend which is on the upswing in all fields of human endeavor is bound to show that all that cannot be simplified to such an extent. In the end, the thesis of the "impossibility of an ideological coexistence" will be remembered as nothing but the curious outgrowth of an aberrant imagination.

Notes

1. Bernhard Häring, *Das Gesetz Christi* [The Law of Christ]. Freiburg im Breisgau, 1958, pp. 193ff.
2. Ibid., p. 193.
3. Michael Serafian, "Der Pilger oder Konzil und Kirche vor der Entscheidung" [The Pilgrim—Council and Church before the Decision]. *rororo aktuell,* November 1964, p. 206.
4. Cf. also Hans Mühlestein, *Die verhüllten Götter* [The Veiled Gods]. Munich 1957.—Though written in a vein of enormous emotional tension, this book offers a remarkable commentary on our subject. See especially the chapter "Ursprung und Geschichte der päpstlichen Machtidee" [Origin and History of the Idea of Papal Power] (pp. 234ff.).
5. Mario von Galli and Bernhard Moosbrugger, *Das Konzil. Chronik der zweiten Session* [The Council. A Report on the Second Session]. Olten, p. 84.
6. From a conversation during the World Peace Congress in Moscow, 1963.
7. Wilfried Daim, *Linkskatholizismus. Eine katholische Initiative in Moskau* [Catholicism of Leftist Orientation. A Catholic Initiative in Moscow]. Europa Verlag (Vienna), 1965.—Id., *Progressiver Katholizismus* [Progressive Catholicism]. Manz (Munich), 1967.
8. Wilfried Daim, *Christentum und Revolution* [Christianity and Revolution]. Manz (Munich), 1967.
9. Ibid.
10. This point was clearly understood already by Alexis de Tocqueville in *L'Ancien régime et la révolution* [The Ancien Régime and the Revolution], 1856.
11. Michael de Fernandy, *Dschingis Chan* [Genghis Khan]. Hamburg, 1958, pp. 150f.
12. Eduard Winter, *Rußland und das Papsttum* [Russia and the Papacy]. Berlin, 1960, I, pp. 97f.
13. Ibid.
14. Ibid., I, p. 287.

15. Ibid., II, p. 281.
16. Cf. *KathPress* of July 24, 1963, No. 170, p. 2.—This report supplies the further information that the relics were returned in 1962 to the Ukrainian Catholic Church of St. Barbara in Vienna. This, however, is an error. They are still in St. Peter's in Rome.
17. The Polish Episcopate, as represented by Cardinal Wyszynski, insists stubbornly that the inadequate supply of paper allotted to it does not permit the introduction of a liturgy in Polish. It is certainly true that allotment restrictions represent in communist countries one of the methods of limiting the impact of unwelcome publications. However, a liturgy existed before the invention of the printing press, and if the Poles were really eager to have a Polish liturgy, they could simply emulate the example of the Czech Church which introduced a Czech liturgy although it has to contend with paper-allotment restrictions of a kind similar to those prevailing in Poland. The line of reasoning of the competent Church agencies may probably be reduced to the following simplified point: If the Council reaches a decision that we dislike but that promotes in one way or another the interest of the Polish government, then that government should make its contribution toward the implementation of the Council's decision, and that would be to provide additional paper. If the Polish government were indeed eager to have a progressive and hence antinationalist development take place in the Church in Poland, it would comply with the request for additional paper. But the communists in Poland have no clear conception of what they want: the total destruction of the Church or a positive cooperation with it. And that is the reason nothing whatsoever is happening.
18. Cited after Maxim Mura's work on the Vatican and the Soviet Union, published in Paris in 1965 (p. 47).
19. Max Lackmann, *Mit evangelischen Augen. Beobachtungen eines Lutheraners auf dem Zweiten vatikanischen Konzil* [Through Protestant Eyes. Observations of a Lutheran as the Second Vatican Council]. Graz-Vienna-Cologne, 1963, I, pp. 63ff.
20. Ibid., p. 324.
21. Ibid., p. 67.
22. Ibid., pp. 318ff.
23. Ibid., pp. 231ff.
24. Tadeusz Breza, *Das eherne Tor. Römische Aufzeichnungen* [The Bronze Gate. Roman Notebook]. Luchterhand (Neuried), pp. 285f.
25. August M. Knoll has repeatedly mentioned to me this statement of Seipel's.

26. Adolf Hitler, *Mein Kampf* [My Struggle].

27. Tadeusz Breza, *op. cit.*, pp. 299ff.

28. Tadeusz Breza, *op. cit.*, p. 569.

29. Wilfried Daim, *Linkskatholizismus* . . . (See 7 above), p. 42.

30. Luke 1, 51–52. Cf. also Wilfried Daim, *Christentum und Revolution* (See 8 above).

31. Michael Serafian, *op. cit.*, p. 11.

32. *Außenpolitik,* February 1966.

33. *Progrès Egyptien* (Cairo), March 8, 1966.

34. In the form of a questionnaire in the periodical *Kirunki* on the occasion of the Polish millennial celebration.

35. A discussion of Cardinal Mindszenty's address from a Hungarian communist point of view may be found in the four volumes of documentation on the events in October 1956 in Hungary, published by the Information Service of the Hungarian Council of Ministers, especially IV, p. 53.

36. Ibid.

37. Cf. Ernst Karl Winter, *Die Sozialmetaphysik der Scholastik* [Social Metaphysics of Scholasticism]. Leipzig and Vienna, 1929.—The findings of this study were exemplified by the same author in *Ignaz Seipel als dialektisches Problem. Ein Beitrag zur Scholastikforschung* [Ignaz Seipel as a Problem in Dialectics. A Contribution to Research in Scholasticism]. Europa Verlag (Vienna), 1966. Cf. also August M. Knoll, *Katholische Kirche und scholastisches Naturrecht. Zur Frage der Freiheit* [The Catholic Church and Scholastic Natural Law. On the Question of Freedom]. Europa Verlag (Vienna), 1962.

38. Personal communication by Friedrich Heer.

39. Tadeusz Breza, *op. cit.*, p. 88.

40. It is extremely difficult to explain to a functionary of the Catholic Church that it is in the interest of his institution to practice self-criticism rather than provoke criticism by others. One might assume that Jesus made the point sufficiently clear in the parable of the mote and the beam.

41. *Hungarian Press Service* X, No. 238, November 28, 1966.

42. Hugh Seton-Watson, *Die osteuropäische Revolution* [The Eastern European Revolution]. Isar Verlag (Munich), 1966, pp. 74f.

43. Lothar Rendulic, *Gekämpft, gesiegt, geschlagen* [Battle, Victory, Defeat].

44. Professor Supek from Zagreb, contributing to the discussion at a round-table conference organized by the Institute of Social Science and Political Information, November 2 to 5, 1966, in Munich, on

the question of "The Message of Hegel, Marx, and Lenin in Its Present-Day Significance."

45. Cf. Wilfried Daim, "Selbstkastration der Autoritäten" [Self-Emasculation of the Authorities]. *Forum* (Vienna), October 1968.

A Check List
of Important Primary Sources*

1. Address of the Papal Legate, Eugenio Cardinal Pacelli, before the Thirty-Fourth International Eucharistic Congress, May 29, 1938, on the Square of Heroes in Budapest, Hungary.
   See: Eugenio Cardinale Pacelli, *Discorsi e Panegirici* (1931–38). Milan, 1949, pp. 743f.

2. Encyclical of John XXIII, *Pacem in terris.*

3. Address by Cardinal D. Franz König presented at Seggau on the occasion of a meeting of the Working Committee for Public Affairs of the organization Catholic Action in the Steiermark.
   See: KathPress, May 12, 1964, No. 109, Supplement 1.

4. Address of Paul VI to the Eleventh National Congress of the Association of Christian Industrialists in Italy, June 8, 1964.
   See: KathPress, Documentation No. 136.

5. Encyclical of Paul VI, *Ecclesiam suam.*

6. Palmiro Togliatti, posthumous memorandum.
   See: Volksstimme (Vienna), September 19, 1964.

7. Luigi Longo, addressing himself to the Catholics.
   See: Unità (Rome), October 8, 1964.

8. "The Old Communism is Dying." Spiegel conversation with the head of the Italian Communist Party, Luigi Longo.
   See: Der Spiegel, No. 36, August 29, 1966.

9. Resolution of the Bishops of the Alchite (Uniat) Church convened under the chairmanship of their patriarch Maximos.
   See: Progrès Egyptien (Cairo), March 8, 1966.

10. Encyclical of Paul VI, *Populorum progressio.*

* Reprinted in full or in part in the German Edition of the present study: Wilfried Daim, *Der Vatikan und der Osten.* Europa Verlag (Vienna), 1967, pp. 173–456.

11. Complaint of two Russian Orthodox priests about state interference with freedom of religion and freedom of conscience.
    See: Frankfurter Allgemeine Zeitung, June 14, 1966.

12. W. Ardatowski, commentator of the Nowosti News Agency (APN), on the USSR and the Vatican.
    See: APN, Moscow, January 17, 1967.

13. Address of Pope John XXIII to the Polish bishops in 1962, as released by the embassy of the People's Republic of Poland in Vienna.

14. Sermon of Stefan Cardinal Wyszynski on the occasion of the twentieth anniversary of the organization of Polish church life in the western and northern territories.
    See: WTK, Tygodnik Katolikow, October 1965.

15. Archbishop Boleslaw Kominek, in the concluding lecture of a series presented at Wroclaw, August 23 to 29, 1965, on the subject of the Church and the Western Territories.
    See: WTK, Tygodnik Katolikow, October 1965.

16. Pastoral letter of the Polish bishops on the occasion of the twentieth anniversary of the organization of Polish church life in the western and northern territories.
    See: WTK, Tygodnik Katolikow, October 1965.

17. Address of the Secretary of the Central Committee of the Polish United Workers Party, Zenon Kliszko, September 15, 1965.
    See: WTK, Tygodnik Katolikow, October 1965.

18. Memorandum of the Evangelical Church in Germany on the situation of the displaced [Germans] from eastern areas and on the relationship of the German people to its eastern neighbors.
    See: Europa Archiv, Series 1, 1966.

19. Message of the Catholic bishops of Poland to the Catholic bishops of Germany, dated November 18, 1965, as transmitted during the Second Ecumenical Council in Rome.
    See: Europa Archiv, Series 1, 1966.

20. Message of the Catholic bishops of Germany to the Catholic bishops of Poland, dated December 5, 1965.
    See: Europa Archiv, Series 1, 1966·

21. Letter of invitation of the Catholic bishops of Poland to the Catholic bishops of Spain.
    See: ABC, Madrid, December 21, 1965.

22. "In Whose Name?"
    See: Zycie Warszawy, December 10, 1965. Also *Polnische Berichte,* Special Edition.

23. Statement of the group of deputies "ZNAK" as read in the Sejm on December 14, 1965, by Jerzy Zawiejski.
    See: Polnische Berichte, Special Edition.

24. Statement of the association "PAX" of December 28, 1965.
    See: Polnische Berichte, Special Edition.

25. Communiqué of the office of the Council of Ministers of the People's Republic of Poland.
    See: Polnische Berichte, Special Edition.

26. Hansjakob Stehle, "Dialog mit Mißverständnissen" [Dialogue Beset with Misunderstandings].
    See: Die Furche, No. 1, 1966.

27. Long-distance telephone conversation of Hansjakob Stehle with Archbishop Boleslaw Kominek.
    See: Die Furche, No. 3, 1966.

28. Address of Wladyslaw Gomulka to the plenary session of the all Polish Committee of the United National Front on January 14, 1966.
    See: Polnische Berichte.

29. Conversation of Kurt Skalnik with Archbishop Boleslaw Kominek.
    See: Die Furche, No. 8, 1966.

30. Position of the Polish Ecumenical Council relative to the message of the Polish Roman Catholic Episcopate to the Roman Catholic Episcopate of Germany.
    See: the Special Brochure published by the Polish Ecumenical Council, Warsaw, 1966.

31. Communication of the Episcopate to the Chairman of the Council of Ministers of the People's Republic of Poland, Josef Cyrankiewicz, dated February 10, 1966.
    See: Polnische Berichte, No. 3, 1966.

32. Pastoral letter of the Polish Episcopate of February 10, 1966.
    See: Polnische Berichte, No. 3, 1966.

33. "'A New Interpretation."
    See: Tribuna Ludu, March 17, 1966.—Also *Polnische Berichte,* No. 3, 1966.

34. Letter of the Secretary of the Episcopate, Zygmunt Choromanski, to Minister Janusz Wieczorek, Chief of the Office of the Council of Ministers.
    See: Polnische Berichte, No. 4, 1966.

35. Letter of the Chief of the Office of the Council of Ministers, Minister Janusz Wieczorek, to Bishop Zygmunt Choromanski, Secretary of the Episcopate.
    See: Polnische Berichte, No. 4, 1966.

36. Letter of invitation of the Polish bishops to the Austrian bishops to attend the Polish millennial celebration.
    See: KathPress, December 14, 1965, No. 289, p. 1.

37. Reply of the Austrian bishops to the invitation of the Polish Episcopate to take part in the millennial celebration of the Christianization of Poland.
    See: KathPress, December 10, 1966, No. 33, Supplement 1.

38. On the position of the archbishops and bishops of Austria relative to the Polish millennial celebration.
    See: Die Furche, No. 19, 1966.

39. Address of Wladislaw Gomulka on the occasion of the Polish millennial celebration in Poznan, April 17, 1966.
    See: Polnische Berichte, No. 4, 1966.

40. On the question of the relations between state and Church.
    See: Nowe Drogi, organ of the Central Committee of the United Polish Workers Party, No. 4, 1966.—Also *Polnische Berichte,* No. 4, 1966.

41. Pastoral letter of Primate Joseph Cardinal Mindszenty of October 18, 1945. The Hungarian original bears the handwritten notation: "Text not released, destroyed." The rest of the note is illegible except for the words "in Nógrád."

42. Address of Cardinal Mindszenty on November 3, 1956, during the Hungarian uprising.

43. Report of the Central Committee to the Ninth Congress of the United Socialist Workers Party, presented by the Secretary of the Central Committee, János Kádár, November 28, 1966.
See: *MTI* (Viennese Edition), No. 228, Appendix, pp. 7f.

44. On the policy of the stretched-out hand, by Frigyes Todero.
See: *Tátsadalmi szemle* (Budapest), No. 2, 1967.—This publication is the theoretical organ of the Hungarian Socialist Workers Party.

45. On the dialogue between Marxists and Christians, by Zdenko Roter.
See: *Kommunist* (Belgrade), May 12, 1966.—Also *Ost-Probleme,* XVIII, No. 11, June 3, 1966, p. 333.

46. On the fruit of realism, relative to the signing of the protocol of the Yugoslav-Vatican conversations, by Branko Skrinjar.
See: *Kommunist* (Belgrade), June 30, 1966.—Also *Ost-Probleme* XIX, No. 3, February 10, 1967.

47. A critical evaluation of the meaning of a dialogue between Marxists and Christians, by Dr. Esad Cimić.
See: *Kommunist* (Belgrade), October 20 and 27, 1966.—Also *Ost-Probleme* XIX, No. 3, February 10, 1967.

48. "Kirche und sozialistischer Staat" [The Church and the Socialist State]. An analysis of the protocol of the conversations between Yugoslavia and the Holy See, by Frane Franic, Bishop of Split.
See: *Die Furche,* No. 6, 1967.

49. An open letter of the Central Committee of the Communist Party of Germany to the Catholics of Germany, June 30, 1936.
See: W. A. Schmidt, *Damit Deutschland lebe* [So that Germany May Live]. Berlin, 1958.

50. Concluding remarks of Walter Ulbricht before the Third National Congress.
See: *Neues Deutschland,* September 24, 1958, p. 5.

51. Policy statement of the Chairman of the State Council, Walter Ulbricht, to the People's Chambers of the German Democratic Republic, October 4, 1960.
See: *Christen und Marxisten verbinden gemeinsame Ziele und Ideale* [Christians and Marxists Have Common Objectives and Ideals]. Berlin, 1961.

52. Replies of Walter Ulbricht made during a conversation with a

delegation of theologians, church dignitaries, and Christian bishops, February 6, 1961.

See: Christen und Marxisten verbinden gemeinsame Ziele und Ideale [Christians and Marxists Have Common Objectives and Ideals]. Berlin, 1961.

53. Statement of the Chairman of the State Council of the German Democratic Republic, Walter Ulbricht, during a conversation at the Wartburg, August 18, 1964.

    See: Marxisten und Christen wirken gemeinsam für Frieden und Humanismus [Marxists and Christians Are Jointly at Work for the Cause of Peace and Humanism]. Berlin, 1964.

54. Address of Walter Ulbricht on the occasion of the Twentieth Anniversary of the Establishment of the Socialist Unity Party of Germany, August 21, 1966.

    See: Der Weg zum künftigen Vaterland der Deutschen [The Road to the Future Fatherland of the Germans]. Dietz (Berlin), 1966.

Index